DELIVERANCE

BY FIRE

21 Days of Word Immersion, and Fire Prayers for Total Healing, Deliverance, Breakthrough, and Divine Intervention

Daniel C. Okpara

Copyright © September 2018 by Daniel C. Okpara.

All Rights Reserved. Kindly note that contents of this book should not be reproduced in any way or by any means without obtaining written consent from the author or his representative. However, brief excerpts for church or Christian references can be used without written permission.

Published By:

Better Life Media.

BETTER LIFE WORLD OUTREACH CENTER.

Website: www.BetterLifeWorld.org

Email: info@betterlifeworld.org

FOLLOW US ON FACEBOOK

1. Like our Page on Facebook for updates

2. Join Our Facebook Prayer Group, submit prayer requests and follow powerful daily prayers for total victory and breakthrough

---

This title and others are available for quantity discounts for sale promotions, gifts, and evangelism. Visit our website or email us to get started.

Any scripture quotation used in this book is taken from the New King James Version, except where stated. Used by permission.

Table of Contents

RECEIVE DAILY AND WEEKLY PRAYERS 9

FREE BOOKS 10

HOW TO USE THIS BOOK 11

INTRODUCTION 16

DAY 1: WHAT IS DELIVERANCE? 21

    WHAT EXACTLY IS DELIVERANCE? 21

    WHY MANY PRAY FOR DELIVERANCE AND DON'T GET IT 24

    PRAYERS 27

DAY 2: WHEN DO YOU NEED DELIVERANCE? 30

    PROBLEMS THAT REQUIRE DELIVERANCE PRAYERS 33

    PRAYERS 40

DAY 3: WHAT CAN OPEN DOORS FOR SATAN IN ONE'S LIFE? 43

    THE LAW OF CAUSE AND EFFECT 48

    PRAYERS 50

DAY 4: HOW TO OBTAIN DELIVERANCE 54

    1. Total Repentance 55

    2. Fasting and Prayer 57

    4. Pray Until You're Free 58

    5. Be Sensitive as You Pray 59

6. Know and Use the Best Hours to Pray 60

PRAYERS 63

DAY 5: UNDERSTANDING OUR TOOLS FOR DELIVERANCE 67

1. The Name of Jesus Christ 69
2. The Blood of Jesus Christ 70
3. The Power of the Holy Communion 72
4. The Power of Declaring Scriptures 73
5. The Weapon of Faith 75
6. The Weapon of Fire 76
6. The Power of the Anointing Oil 77

PRAYERS 78

DAY 6: DEALING WITH SATANIC STRONGHOLDS 81

IDENTIFYING STRONGHOLDS 84
ATTACKING THE STRONGHOLDS 87
DECLARE YOUR VICTORY EVERY DAY 87
PRAYERS 88

DAY 7: DEALING WITH NEGATIVE SOUL TIES, AGREEMENTS AND VOWS 93

WHAT ARE SOUL TIES? 94
NEGATIVE AGREEMENTS AND ALLIANCES 99
UNFULFILLED VOWS AND PLEDGES 100
PRAYERS 102

DAY 8: KILLING GOLIATH: THE SPIRIT OF FEAR..........109

- A LESSON FROM THE FALL OF JERICHO 111
- FEAR OPENS DOOR FOR EVIL................................114
- THE COMMAND TO FEAR NOT 116
- WHAT YOU FEAR, YOU CREATE 117
- PRAYERS...119

DAY 9: KILLING JEZEBEL: THE SPIRIT OF WITCHCRAFT...............125

- WHAT THE BIBLE SAYS ABOUT WITCHCRAFT 127
- TYPES OF WITCHCRAFT 132
- HOW TO KNOW IF YOU'RE UNDER A WITCHCRAFT ATTACK......143
- PRAYERS...147

DAY 10: KILLING PHARAOH: STUBBORN DESTINY CHASERS.......157

- AFFLICTION FROM CHILDHOOD................................158
- HARDNESS OF HEART 159
- RECURRENT AFFLICTION..160
- THE SPIRIT OF MOCKERY AND ARROGANCE...............162
- PHARAOHS ARE GODS 163
- EMPLOYMENT OF SORCERERS 163
- EMOTIONAL HARASSMENT.....................................164
- OPPRESSION - HARD LABOR 165
- PURSUERS UNTO DEATH 165
- HOW TO PRAY THROUGH THE SPIRIT OF PHARAOH 166
- PRAYERS...169

DAY 11: OVERCOMING THE FORCES OF DELAY AND DENIAL......173

UNDERSTANDING WHEN DELAYS ARE FROM GOD 173

UNDERSTANDING SATANIC DELAYS...176

DANIEL AND THE PRINCE OF PERSIA 177

JACOB AND LABAN 179

PAUL AND SATAN 180

DELAYED FOR 38 YEARS..181

CAUSES OF DEMONIC DELAYS..182

HOW TO BREAK THE POWERS OF DELAY AND DENIAL 187

PRAYERS...188

DAY 12: DEALING WITH THE SPIRITS OF INFIRMITY 193

1. CAUSING PHYSICAL HEALTH PROBLEMS................................197

2. CAUSING EMOTIONAL DISORDER 198

OPEN DOORS FOR THE DEMONS OF INFIRMITY 198

PRAYERS...200

DAY 13: PRAYING AGAINST THE FORCES OF INJUSTICE..............204

STORY 1: FOR RUSHING NEIGHBOR TO THE HOSPITAL, MAN SPENDS TWO YEARS IN PRISON 204

STORY 2: INNOCENT MAN DEMANDS £1M COMPENSATION AFTER SPENDING 17 YEARS IN JAIL FOR LOOKALIKE'S CRIME 205

PRAYERS...208

DAY 14: DELIVERANCE FROM FINANCIAL HARDSHIP 213

PRAYING AGAINST FINANCIAL DEMONS 216

PRAYERS 221

PRAYER 1 – SURRENDER 223

PRAYER 2 – POWER TO OBEY 224

PRAYER 3 – REBUKE THE DEVIL 226

PRAYER 4 – DIVINE IDEAS AND DIRECTION 228

DAY 15: WAR AGAINST ANTI-MARRIAGE SPIRITS 231

PRAYERS 234

DAY 16: DREAM ROBBERS 246

USING YOUR DREAMS TO FIGHT YOUR BATTLES 248

WHAT TO DO WITH YOUR DREAMS 251

PRAYERS 253

DAY 17: THE POWER OF PARENTAL BLESSINGS 257

DON'T PLAY WITH PARENTAL BLESSINGS 259

HONOR YOUR PARENTS 262

BLESS YOUR CHILDREN NO MATTER WHAT 263

PRAYERS 264

DAY 18: DELIVERANCE OF THE TONGUE 268

PRAYERS 272

DAY 19: BREAKING THE CURSE OF DEBT 276

WHY YOU'RE IN DEBT 277

GOD'S WORD ON DEBT 279
HOW TO BE FREE FROM DEBT 282
PRAYERS...287

DAY 20: A PRAYER OF AGREEMENT AGAINST SPECIFIC OPPRESSIONS **290**

PRAYERS...292

DAY 21: THE POWER OF PRAISE IN DELIVERANCE......................**294**

PRAYERS...298

ENDING PRAYER **301**

ADDENDUM: HOW TO MAINTAIN YOUR DELIVERANCE............**302**

1. PRACTICE ADVANCE FORGIVENESS 303
2. ALLOW NO VACUUM IN YOUR MIND........................304
3. GET BUSY FOR GOD 304
4. LEARN TO EXERCISE YOUR AUTHORITY AND FAITH 305
6. USE YOUR WORDS RIGHT 305

GET IN TOUCH..**307**

OTHER BOOKS BY THE SAME AUTHOR **308**

ABOUT THE AUTHOR **311**

NOTES..**311**

RECEIVE DAILY AND WEEKLY PRAYERS

Powerful Prayers Sent to Your Inbox Every Monday

Enter your email address to receive notifications of new posts, prayers and prophetic declarations sent to you by email.

Email Address

Sign Me Up

Go to: ***www.BreakThroughPrayers.org*** *to subscribe to receive FREE WEEKLY PRAYER POINTS, and prophetic declarations sent to you by email.*

FREE BOOKS ...

Download These 4 Powerful Books Today for FREE... Take Your Relationship With God to a New Level.

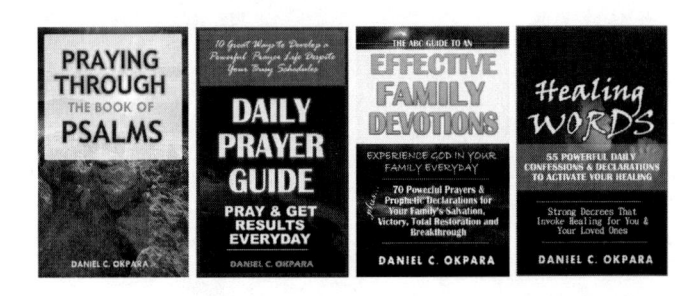

www.betterlifeworld.org/grow

How to Use This Book

Kindly Read this Bible Passage Carefully

₆*Is not this the fast that I have chosen? To loose the bands of wickedness, to undo the heavy burdens, and to let the oppressed go free, and that ye break every yoke?*

₇*Is it not to deal thy bread to the hungry, and that thou bring the poor that are cast out to thy house? When thou seest the naked, that thou cover him; and that thou hide not thyself from thine own flesh?*

₈*Then shall thy light break forth as the morning, and thine health shall spring forth speedily: and thy righteousness shall go before thee; the glory of the Lord shall be thy reward.*

₉*Then shalt thou call, and the Lord shall answer; thou shalt cry, and he shall say, Here I am. If thou take away from the midst of thee the yoke, the putting forth of the finger, and speaking vanity;* ₁₀ *and if thou draw out thy soul to the hungry, and satisfy the afflicted soul; then shall thy light rise in obscurity, and thy darkness be as the noonday:*

[11] And the Lord shall guide thee continually, and satisfy thy soul in drought, and make fat thy bones: and thou shalt be like a watered garden, and like a spring of water, whose waters fail not.

This book is a twenty-one-day fasting and prayer guide for all-around deliverance and breakthroughs. These teachings and prayers will touch every aspect of your life and provoke great transformations. Your health will be restored. Your finances will be healed, and you will experience breakthroughs. You will find a job. Your home will experience a great spiritual transformation, and your marriage will be restored. You will experience great peace.

Please carefully follow these instructions as you pray these prayers:

1. Read the contents day by day. Don't rush it. It's a daily reading and prayer manual. Read it one day at a time, and digest the teachings.

2. Endeavor to pray all the prayers for each day. There are many prayers for each day. Pray them, and then more. Don't be limited to the prayer words. Let them direct and guide you. As you begin to pray, follow your heart and pray other points you're inspired to pray.

3. Read and meditate on the recommended further reading scriptures. There are Bible references at the end of each day, recommended to be read in addition to the prayers and teachings of the day. Endeavor to read these scriptures, meditate on them, and pray their revelations.

4. Important: Pray for others. In addition to praying these personal prayers for yourself, please pray for others. Make a list of people to intercede for during these 21 days, and earnestly pray for them. Our website also receives hundreds of specific prayer requests daily. Please visit the prayer requests board and help pray for these requests. Here's the link:

www.betterlifeworld.org/prayer-requests-board.

Praying for others is a major instruction that we follow in our ministry each time we are seeking the Lord, because we believe that what you help achieve in the lives of others, God inspires others to make in your own life.

5. On day five we talked about the best hours you should pray. While you can read that later, we recommend that you pray mainly in the midnight hours. Spend at least one hour in prayer each day for this next twenty-one days.

6. What kind of fasting should you do? There is no specific type of fasting that we recommend. You may skip breakfast and lunch if you can. And if you can't, it's okay. If what you can afford is to skip one meal a day, that's acceptable.

Skipping dinner to pray is also a very effective fast you should try. It means you can go about your business during the day and hook up with God in the night hours.

Here are some fasting you can do with this prayer guide:

- 6:00 am to 10 am
- 6 am to noon
- 6 am – 3 pm
- 6 am – 6 pm
- 6 pm – 6 am

We encourage people to drink water while fasting. If you're embarking on a long fast, such as three days dry fast, we recommend that you drink water and juice. The reason is that you're not on a hunger strike. You are waiting on the LORD, and you'll need physical strength to pray and listen to the Holy Spirit.

> **What makes a good fast is spending quality hours in Bible study, and prayers.**

Expect great supernatural intervention as you seek God.

Introduction

Praying With Fire: Is it Biblical?

"For our God is a consuming fire." – Heb. 12:29

Fire in the Bible is not only a representation of hell. It also represents a wide range of things – both literal and symbolic. Here's a list of selected ways the concept of fire is used in the Bible.

- Used for daily activities, such as cooking, keeping warm, giving light, or burning trash (See Exo 12:8; John 21:9, Isaiah 44:15; John 18:18), Isaiah 50:11; Matt. 25:1-13), Leviticus 8:17).

- Used for refining metals, such as silver and gold (Numbers 31:22–23; Malachi 3:2–3),

- Used to destroy enemy's cities in war (Joshua 6:24; 8:8; 11:11; Judges 1:8; 1 Kings 9:16; Mt 22:7)

- Used as a means for executing sentenced criminals (Daniel 3; Genesis 38:24; Leviticus 20:14; 21:9; Joshua 7:15)

- Used to burn sacrifices in the Temple (Leviticus 2:2; 6:8–13)

- A manifestation of God's presence: E.g., the burning bush, Mt. Sinai, the pillar of fire, God surrounded by fire (See Exodus 3:2, 12: 21, 19:18, Numbers 14:14, Ezekiel 1:27)

- Used as punishment: e.g., Sodom and Gomorrah, disobedient priests, and enemies (Gen. 19:24, Leviticus 10:1-2, Revelation 20:9, Ezekiel 38:22; 39:6).

- God's present-day judgment is often symbolized as destruction by fire (See Psalm 97:3; Isaiah 33:12; Joel 2:3; Micah 1:4)

- God's coming, and final judgment is depicted as fire (2 Thessalonians 1:7; Revelation 8:7-8, 9:17–18, 18:8)

- Used for judging the prophets of Baal(1 Kings 18:20-40)

- Fire is a beautiful picture of the work of the Holy Spirit. He brings God's presence, God's passion, and God's purity ((Matthew 3:11).

As you can see, God's consuming fire has some very significant applications. In this book, we shall be applying God's fire as a tool of judgment on the works of the wicked and for our purification. As a tool of judgment on the works of the wicked, we shall be claiming our freedom from all forms of demonic harassments by fire – That is what I call *Deliverance by Fire*. And as an instrument of purification, we shall be engaging God's fire for our complete cleansing, spiritual restoration, and renewal.

Are you ready to stop the devil in your life and family today?

Are you ready to say enough is enough to all forms of Satan-instigated threats against your marriage, children, finances, health, and divine purpose?

Are you ready to claim God's promises for your business, career, marriage, and life? Are you willing to say never until you see His promises?

I'm calling you for 21 days of intensive fire prayers against every evil harassment in your life and family. I am confident that as you go through the eye-opening teachings in this book and embark on the prayers, whatever unjust circumstances in your life right now will bow.

You will experience supernatural intervention in the most challenging situations of your life as you pray these prayers and wait on the Lord.

Deliverance by Fire

The Bible says: ₁₀*And now also the ax is laid unto the root of the trees: consequently every tree which brings not forth good fruit is hewn down and cast into the fire.*

₁₁ I indeed baptize you with water unto repentance. But he that cometh after me is mightier than I, whose shoes I am not worthy to bear: **he shall baptize you with the Holy Ghost, and with fire***: ₁₂ Whose fan is in his hand, and he will thoroughly purge his floor, and gather his wheat into the garner, but he will burn up the chaff with unquenchable fire.*
- Matthew 3:10-12

....

Say with me:

Heavenly Father, I come before You today for a new baptism. I ask for the Baptism of the Holy Spirit and Fire. Let every chaff in me be burned up and destroyed from today onwards. May every thought, idea, and attitude in me which does not bear the right fruits be hewn down and cast into the fire.

Let Your fire, Lord, consume every seed of stubbornness and disobedience in me. By Your fire, Lord, draw me unto repentance and a new fervent walk with You. And grant me total deliverance as I

seek You going forward, in the unchallengeable name of Jesus Christ.

It's time to call down fire from heaven. It's time to invoke God's fire of judgment on the wicked works of darkness. It's time to demand your deliverance and refuse nothing else until you're free. You have suffered enough. You have hidden enough. It's time to challenge all prophets of Baal against your life and show them that our God is a consuming fire.

Day 1: What is Deliverance?

*₇And the Lord said, 'I have surely seen the oppression of My people who are in Egypt and have heard their cry because of their taskmasters, for I know their sorrows. ₈**So I have come down to deliver them out of the hand of the Egyptians**, and to bring them up from that land to a good and vast land, to a land flowing with milk and honey, to the place of the Canaanites and the Amorites and the Hittites and the Hivites and the Perizzites and the Jebusites.*

₉Now, therefore, see, the cry of the children of Israel has come to Me, and I have also seen the oppression with which the Egyptians oppress them. 10 Come now, therefore, and I will send you to Pharaoh that you may bring My people, the children of Israel, out of Egypt." - Exodus 3:7-9

WHAT EXACTLY IS DELIVERANCE?

You need to know what deliverance means before embarking on prayers for deliverance. As I've said from time to time, what most people assume that *deliverance* means is not indeed what it is. For instance, *deliverance* is not necessarily about casting out of demons or doing spiritual warfare prayers. It is not falling under the anointing during ministrations, crusades, or prophetic services. Deliverance is not demons speaking through someone and people running around. Deliverance is not a new doctrine that creates confusion.

According to the scripture we just read, *deliverance* is God saving his people from their oppression, pains, unjust persecutions, dangers, and distresses, and leading them to His promises for their lives. **It is being free from one's bondage and limitations and empowered to fulfill God's purpose for one's life.** So if the prayers and *fallings* do not produce freedom from one's unjust burdens, pains, and sufferings, deliverance has not taken place.

In the Old Testament, deliverance is seen as God saving his people from their troubles or giving them victory over their enemies. In the New Testament, deliverance is:

=> Being saved from sin (through faith in Christ)

=> Being set free from evil spirits oppression and possession

=> Healing from sicknesses and diseases

=> Being saved from trials and ungodly persecution

=> Being saved from danger, troubles or death.

So when we say, **deliverance**, you don't begin to say, *"Well, I ain't got no demons in me."*

As children of God, we may pray and seek deliverance from God regarding any situation that is unpleasing and limiting us from being the best for the kingdom of God here on earth.

I define deliverance as a supernatural intervention in human affairs that stops the activities of the wicked and empowers God's people to walk out of their undesirable situations and begin their journey to fulfilling their God-given assignment

---

Deliverance is usually an expression of God's love and mercy, not something we deserve.

There are three powerful forces involved in the process of deliverance. They are:

=> God's love

=> Christ's compassion

=> The power of the Holy Spirit.

We do not obtain deliverance from the oppression of demons or wicked individuals because we know how to pray, shout or cry. We obtain deliverance because God's love is extended towards us without measure.

> God did not even spare his own Son for us but gave him up for us all, won't he also surely give us everything else, including deliverance, healing, and peace? – Rom. 8:32 (Paraphrased)

As you begin to seek deliverance from whatever negative situation you're experiencing in your life at the moment, have confidence that your prayers will be answered. The price for your total freedom has been paid fully at the Cross. We're not trying to struggle for our freedom; we're only enforcing it standing on the Word of God and His promises.

WHY MANY PRAY FOR DELIVERANCE AND DON'T GET IT

As we proceed in this prayer quest, we will undoubtedly touch many areas and many issues to deal with to obtain your deliverance. But it boils down to the fact is that deliverance is achieved by adhering to God's word.

We take time to teach the Word before prayers because I have learned that we're not heard by the multitude of our prayers. **Praying without knowledge can lead to frustration.** That's why we must spend the time to listen, read, digest and pray in the Word first.

The Bible says:

Hosea 4: 5-6 - *Therefore you shall stumble in the day; the prophet also shall stumble with you in the night, and I will destroy your mother. My people are destroyed for lack of knowledge. Because you have rejected knowledge, I also will reject you from being priest for Me; because you have forgotten the law of your God, I also will forget your children.*

Isaiah 5:13 - *Therefore my people have gone into captivity because they have no knowledge; their honorable men are famished, and their multitude dried up with thirst.*

Job 36-12: *But if they do not obey, they shall perish by the sword, and they shall die without knowledge.*

Jeremiah 5:4 - *Therefore I said, "Surely these are poor. They are foolish; for they do not know the way of the Lord, the judgment of their God."*

....

All of these scriptures are referring to God's people. They stumble in the day, not because they are not praying and receiving prophetic messages and prophetic words of knowledge. As Hosea says, they stumble, and their prophets also stumble with them. That is, even the ones giving them prophecies are also stumbling with them. They will give them predictions; they will wait and wait, nothing. The real prophets will be wondering why their prophecies are not happening, while the **stomach-motivated** prophets will say, *"well, we're all the same. None of us has answers, so let's just do business."*

According to these scriptures, God's people perish, are poor, go into captivity, their honorable men are famished, their multitudes dried up with thirst - not because they are not praying, not because they are not fasting, not because they are not giving and sowing seeds of faith - but because they lack knowledge. They do not know the Word of God, or because they reject it.

There may be many churches and thousands and thousands of preachers, but the word of God is lacking. And until we desire, discover and surrender to the Word, we will continue to stumble, even in the daytime.

I advise you to stop running up and down and settle down with the Word of God. Read it until your heart receives instruction. That's the key to your deliverance.

PRAYERS

Heavenly Father, I thank You because it is Your will for me to be delivered completely from everything that represents demonic activity in my life. I thank You because You will keep your promise in my life, in Jesus name.

I thank You, Jesus, for paying the price for my deliverance. I am not struggling to be delivered, for it is not by my power, not by much prayer, not by might, and not by my efforts that I obtain God's promises. I have already been delivered through Your finished work. I am only enforcing my victory through prayers. For this I say, thank You, Lord, in Jesus name.

Father Lord, You did not spare Your only begotten Son but gave Him up for me, how much more will You set me free from the works of darkness. Thank You Heavenly Father, in Jesus name.

O Lord, I thank You in advance for my deliverance. I know that as I pray, You will guide me and set me free from all of these limitations and empower me to become profitable for Your kingdom and for my family. For this, I say thank You, in Jesus name.

I believe that Jesus Christ is the Son of God. He is My Only Lord and personal Savior. Therefore I overcome the world and the evil in it, in Jesus name.

Thank You, Lord, for the weapons of our warfare that are not carnal but mighty through Christ to pulling down every stronghold and every high thing that exalts itself against the knowledge of God. I thank You that I have all that I need to pray and obtain victory in every aspect of my life, in Jesus name.

I declare today that the LORD is my rock, my fortress, and my deliverer; He is my God and my pillar, in whom I take refuge, my armor and the horn of my salvation. He is my stronghold, my refuge, and my savior. He will save me from violent people and troublous situations, in Jesus name.

Thank You, Lord for giving me the authority that I now possess to tread on serpents and scorpions, and the ability to exercise authority over all the power of the enemy and nothing will in any way harm me, in Jesus name.

Yes, Lord, I am ready for my deliverance. I desire complete freedom from every yoke of darkness preventing me from being the best that You have made me to be. O Lord, deliver me completely and empower me to be the best for YOU, in Jesus name.

Amen

FOR FURTHER READING

Exodus chapter 3 and chapter 4

Day 2: When Do You Need Deliverance?

For we wanted to come to you – I, Paul, again and again, wanted to come, but Satan hindered us. - 1 Thess. 2:18 - AMP

As I said earlier, deliverance includes freedom from every evil work of darkness against your life. It also involves calling forth for justice to be done against wrong events in your life.

In the scripture above, Paul understood that the opposition that stopped his course was from Satan. He fully understood the place of spiritual warfare against the forces of Satan trying hard to hinder God's promises for our lives. The process of standing on God's Words and in prayers to nullify every evil opposition against your life is also deliverance.

In the King James Version, the first time the word *"deliverance"* was mentioned, it was not about casting out of demons. It was about preservation from famine.

In Genesis 45:6-7, Joseph said to his brethren: ₆*For these two years, the hunger has been in the land, and there are still five years in which there will be neither plowing nor harvesting.* ₇

And God sent me ahead of you to preserve a posterity for you in the earth, and to save your lives by **a great deliverance**.

Deliverance here means being saved from famine. That is more like being rescued from the economic crisis.

As I've said over and over, while evil spirits may not possess a Christian, a Christian can be oppressed, tormented, attacked or resisted by demons. Whereas demon possession is the process whereby an evil spirit controls a person, in part or whole, demonic oppression is the unjust abuse, maltreatment, and torment of a person by evil spirits.

A Christian may face coordinated attacks from demonic spirits, such that he will have so many hindrances, restrictions and multiple setbacks that prevent him from receiving healing, spiritual or physical breakthrough. This is possible because we are in ongoing warfare. The devil, the arch-enemy of God and man, is doing all he can to cause men to lose faith in God's love.

Jesus said in John 10:10 that: *'The thief comes to steal, to kill and to destroy."* The Apostle Peter said: *"Be careful—watch out for attacks from Satan, your great enemy. He prowls around like a hungry, roaring lion, looking for some victim to tear apart* (1 Peter 5:8 - TLB).

We have an adversary who is fighting hard to stop believers through various means. So deliverance is also the process of enacting our victory in Christ through prophetic (WORD) warfare. We stand on the God's WORD and speak to the devils and their perceived works to cease operation in Jesus name. We prayerfully locate what may have opened the door for the oppression we are sensing and close them.

We are not to be ignorant of the devices of the devil. He and his demons will probably try at different times to attack our health, finances, relationships, thoughts, etc. He did it to the early Christians. He is trying to do it to us. Stopping these wicked activities is also deliverance.

The Bible says:

> ***"This charge I commit unto thee, son Timothy, according to the prophecies which went before on thee, that thou by them mightest war a good warfare."*** - *1 Timothy 1:18*

Timothy is not here. So the Bible is undoubtedly talking to you and me. It says that we should use the Word of God to make warfare against all the projections, make-believe and lies of the enemy.

PROBLEMS THAT REQUIRE DELIVERANCE PRAYERS

Here are some of the evil manifestations in a person's life that can signal a demonic attack and a need for deliverance:

=> **Uncontrollable sinning against your will:** Uncontrollable anger; uncontrollable lust; overwhelming urge to commit murder, or commit suicide; overpowering behaviors like cutting, biting, stealing, and so on, are almost always a sign of a demonic problem

=> **Mental torment:** Unusual Fear, depression, unfounded sadness in the soul, hearing strange voices in mind that mock, intimidate, accuse, threaten or attempt to bargain; hearing voices that nobody else hears, compulsive thoughts, insanity, frequent panic attacks, mental illness, obsessive, unreasonable anxiety and so on, are signs of a demonic problem.

=> **Severe emotional problems:** such a feeling of rejection for no reason, too frequent low moments and mental breakdowns, obsession with the past, or inability to move on even after many years of losing something, obsessive, uncontrollable, bombardment of thoughts, etc. In this case, however, more than just prayers for deliverance is needed; inner healing must also take place as well as tearing down strongholds.

=> **Unexplainable low mental performance:** such as extreme sleeplessness, or sleepiness, having frequent nightmares, memory loss, confusion, losing interest in things too quickly even after the initial excitement, etc. These situations need deliverance.

=> **Physical health problems:** Constant physical health problems; frequent hospital appointments. God did not create you to live the significant part of your life in hospitals, or to spend a more substantial portion of your income on treatments. If you or your family members are moving from one case of health issue to the other, leading to too frequent hospital time and money, then you need deliverance.

=> **Symptoms such as choking sensations,** pains that seem to move around and for which there is no medical cause, the feeling of tightness about the head or eyes, dizziness, blackouts, or faintings.

=> **Strange desires and feelings:** Sexual attraction towards animals (bestiality), strange sexual appetites, unusually dangerous attractions towards somebody who is married or past lover (soul ties), persistent sexual attraction to a family member (incest), addiction to pornography, sodomy (lesbianism and homosexuality), adulterous tendencies, especially when traced also to happen with other members of the family, past or present. These are demonic situations and strongholds that needs deliverance prayers to handle.

=> **Strange experiences:** such as hearing or feeling movements without seeing anyone; losing things from time to time; household items or properties always disappearing or breaking in strange ways, feeling of being followed or monitored, etc. These are signs of demonic problems.

=> **Prone to wounds**, always having persistent, chronic injuries, accidents, wounds, bruises, cuts, sores, boils.

=> **Sudden personality and attitude** change – severe contrast, schizophrenia, bipolar disorder

=> **Always experiencing unexplainable loss** of things from time to time; loss of hair; loss of money; loss of property; loss of loved ones, and so on.

=> **An obsession** with the occult world, demons, witchcraft and dark creatures, such as wolves, owls, etc. can indicate demonic bondage.

=> **Unexplainable persistent preoccupation with death** is a sure sign of demonic bondage.

=> **An emotional disorder** such as regular outbursts of anger, high and low emotional levels, depressions, constant irresistible fear, persistent feeling of hopelessness, abnormal fixations, etc. are all signs of demonic resistance

=> **Lineages have comparable problems:** If both you and one or more of your past generations have the same kind of problems, then you need deliverance.

=> **Recurring, hereditary family sicknesses**, health problems traced to other members of the family and relatives, past or present.

=> **Generational sins and habits:** such as lying, fraudulent tendencies, alcoholism, practicing sexual pervasion for which one is not able to break free no matter how one innocently tries.

=> **Infertility problems** often found to also happen to other members of the family, such as barrenness, impotence, erectile dysfunction, female issues – such as continual unexplainable infections, hormone problems, menstrual problems, PMS, cramps, fibroids, painful sex, barrenness, miscarriages, cysts, tumors, bladder problems, kidney stones, etc.

=>**Unusual marital problems**, such as severe delays in finding a spouse, family divisions, divorce, polygamous tendencies, inability to settle down in marriage, moving from one partner to another too frequently, an unprecedented series family crisis from time to time, rebellious children, etc.

=> **Unable to have a breakthrough:** unjustifiable financial lack in spite of several years of hard work, prayers and committed giving to God; continual financial crisis for which there is no justifiable reason; unable to find favor with people; having to work so hard with no commensurate results; always experiencing disappointments at the brink of success; living from hand to mouth; always taken advantage of by people in business dealings; sometimes numerous things go wrong all very quickly, and it causes great financial strain, and so on. These are signs of demonic resistance.

=> *"Debtorcracy"* (Deuteronomy 28:47-48), that is, being a slave to borrowing and debts, unable to get out of debt no matter how the person tries, not able to account for monies given or received, uncontrollable squandering and wasting of resources before realizing what is happening, addicted to get-rich-quick schemes, and so on.

=> **Severe low self-esteem** (Deuteronomy 28:43-44) often as a result of abuse, being spoiled, betrayed, or fear. Losing internal freedom to be oneself, can't make own decisions, always afraid to speak out, even when used and abused, always feeling and living like a caged person.

=> **Prone to hate:** people just hate you for no outward reason; you're always getting punished for offenses you didn't commit; whatever you do, no one sees it as good; your good works don't seem to be noticed, no matter how you try; instead of you getting a raise, you get queries. This is a sign of demonic oppression

=> **Persistent nightmares and dreams,** such as consistently seeing oneself in the water or rivers in dreams, always being chased and struggling to survive in dreams, regularly having cats and dogs related dreams, consistently dreaming and seeing oneself in old places, ruins, mother's or father's ancestral homes, always writing exams in dreams or always seeing oneself in former school settings. Dreams or nightmares that are of a horrific nature and often recurring, causing fear (often having demonic images). Usually when these kinds of dreams are repeated over and over, irrespective of one's prayers to stop them, then a more in-depth search is required. Most likely, a spiritual attack is responsible for the situation.

=> **Invasion of the spirit of sadness:** When you suddenly start getting depressed, feeling hopeless, discouraged and separated, you need deliverance prayers.

=> **Unusual disagreements:** when you suddenly start having severe conflicts in your home, family members suddenly become intolerant of one another leading to constant fights, operation, you need deliverance prayers.

=> Additionally, if you suspect that something is wrong somewhere, but you can't lay hold of what it is exactly, then there may be a demonic restriction somewhere.

....

This list may not be exhaustive, but it's enough to help you discern a situation in your life that is a result of demonic activity and not just normal problem. If you can relate with any of the issues raised so far, buckle up and let's enforce your victory in Christ. Be rest assured that there is deliverance for you no matter what the situation is. God's power is available to stop the works of the devil and his demons in your life and family.

For we do not fight against flesh and blood, but against principalities, against powers, against the rulers of the darkness of this age, against spiritual hosts of wickedness in the heavenly places. - Ephesians 6:12 (KJV)

Something may be happening to you, in you or in your family and somehow, something in you is persuaded that this is not right. This is not how things are supposed to be. You may sense some cloud of darkness hovering. Your prayers seem to be hitting the walls, and things keep getting messier. It is a clear sign of spiritual attack that needs deliverance to handle. It's time to obtain deliverance by fire.

PRAYERS

1. Write out all the problems in your life right now that needs to be settled by fire.

2. Drop the paper on the ground and begin to praise and worship God in truth and in spirit. Spend a long time singing, glorifying, and praising God.

Pray:

3. *O Lord, manifest by fire and destroy anything that has vowed that I will not obtain my deliverance and breakthrough, in Jesus name.*

4. *Fire from above, crush every satanic hindrance in my life right now in the name of Jesus Christ.*

5. *Every spiritual thief stealing from my life and family, perish by fire, in the name of Jesus Christ.*

6. *Every evil, hungry beast chasing after my life and destiny, I slay you by fire today, in the name of Jesus Christ.*

7. By the Blood of Jesus Christ, I am coming out of every pit where there is no water; I am coming out of the gross darkness and entering into my days of light and breakthrough in Jesus name.

8. O Lord, as I pray and wait on You, let my deliverance, healing and breakthrough manifest by fire, in Jesus name.

9. Every wall standing between me and my deliverance, healing, peace, and advancement, collapse by fire today, in Jesus name

10. I speak to all these problems on this paper, before the end of this 21 days, I will see you no more. I will look for you, but you will no longer be there, in Jesus name.

11. O Lord, arise and fight these battles on my behalf and give me victory, that Your name may be glorified in my life, in Jesus name.

12. Whom the Lord sets free is free indeed. This is my hour of freedom, and nothing will stop it, in Jesus name

FOR FURTHER READING

Psalm 34:17 - The righteous cry out and the LORD hears them; he delivers them from all their troubles.

Psalm 50:15 - *Call upon Me in the day of trouble; I will deliver you, and you shall glorify Me.*

Psalm 107:6 - *Then they cried out to the LORD in their trouble, and he delivered them from their distress.*

1 John 5:4-5 - *4 For everyone born of God overcomes the world. This is the victory that has overcome the world, even our faith. 5 Who is it that overcomes the world? Only the one who believes that Jesus is the Son of God.*

2 Samuel 22:2-3 - *2 He said: "The LORD is my rock, my fortress, and my deliverer; 3 my God is my rock, in whom I take refuge, my shield and the horn of my salvation. He is my stronghold, my refuge, and my savior— from violent people you save me.*

John 10:9-11 - *9 I am the gate; anyone who enters through me will be saved. They will come in and go out, and find pasture. 10 The thief comes only to steal, kill and destroy; I have come that they may have life, and have it to the full.*

Day 3: Open Doors for Satan

₂₅ You shall burn the carved and sculpted images of their gods in the fire. You shall not crave the silver or gold that is on them, nor take it for yourselves so that you will not be ensnared by it [in a deadly trap], for it is an abomination (repulsive) to the Lord your God.

₂₆ You shall not carry an abomination (idol) into your house, and like it come under the embargo (doomed to destruction); you shall utterly detest, and you shall entirely hate it, for it is something banned. – **Deut. 7:25-26 (AMP)**

God is saying here that the Israelites could come under a curse and suffer if they bring into their houses things used for idol worship. Things like books, drawings, replicas, and so on.

There is a story in Joshua chapter 7 that explains this point. The Israelites had been defeated in a battle by a tiny country called Ai. The whole army, nation, and Joshua were put off.

They went to seek the face of God. And God said: *"So get started. Sanctify the people. Tell them: Get ready for tomorrow by purifying yourselves. For this is what God, the God of Israel, says:* **There are cursed things in the camp. You won't be able to face your enemies until you have gotten rid of these cursed things**. – Joshua 7:13 (TLB)

As long as they had some accursed things with them, they won't be able to face their enemies. What were those things? They were things dedicated to heathen gods. It was later discovered that a man among them, Achan, had stolen those stuff and buried them in his house.

Demonic doorways or open doors are things that give evil spirits access to operating in a person's life. They are legal openings of demons into a person's house, property or life. These things could be…

- Disregarding God's leading constantly (knowingly or unknowingly)

- Walking out of God's will for one's life (such as the case of Naomi and family)

- Existing evil ancestral covenants (often unknown until one asks serious questions)

- Dishonoring parents

- Constant use of foul, negative words over self

- Witchcraft projections (evil-minded individuals using satanic powers to create harm and pain

- Addiction to pornography

- Adultery and sexual pervasion

- Consulting witch doctors, spiritists, voodoo, fortunetellers, palm readers, etc

- Willfully committing fraud

- Past involvement in the occult, freemason, lodge, Eckankar, Rosci cruces, Hare Krishna, etc

- Being involved with false religious organizations that do not accept the Deity of Christ – Jesus is the only way to God.

- Keeping statues, graven images, and accursed figurines (dolls) in one's home

- Having too many pictures of dead people around. There's nothing wrong with memorial photos, but having images of the dead all over the house connotes shrine.

- Financial unfaithfulness

- Occult books, covenanted rings, objects used in witchcraft, satanic movies, and even objects.

- Having hands laid on you by deceitful, fake prophets, or preachers who have compromised their faith in Christ, who have gone into mermaid worship, spiritism, sorcery, and other forms of occult practices so that they can see visions. Yes, you may not know that these people have left the faith; you may not know they are using occult powers to spread their messages. But it doesn't cancel the fact that when they lay hands on you, they are not imparting the Spirit of God, but demonic spirits. Their spiritual impartation in you will be a doorway for demons to work against you. That is why God's word tells us to test every spirit and not run up and down looking for visions and prophecies.

- Soul ties and unhealthy relationships, such as unscriptural, unsupported business agreements, sexual relations with demonically possessed people, etc.

- Past covenants, agreements or binding deals that were not kept.

- Un-kept vows and promises

- Using items dedicated to demons (knowingly or unknowingly)

- Generational curse (problems from one's family lineage identified to still exist. For example, an only son, having an only son, etc.

- Dream attacks, such as eating witchcraft foods in the dream, persistent sexual intercourse in the dream, or physically,

- Drug or alcohol abuse

- Lack of rest

- Excessive fear

- Traumatic events in one's life
- etc.

THE LAW OF CAUSE AND EFFECT

Some people call it the law of mutual exchange; while some call it the law of reciprocity. Whichever you chose, the idea is that for every effect there is a precise cause, likewise for every cause, there is a particular effect.

It is possible that one's actions or inactions, thoughts, words, statements or decrees are the opening of demons to come and oppress a person or a home. It's also likely that none of the sins mentioned above are the reason for a person experiencing high-level spiritual resistance. For instance, in the case of Paul, we do not have any scriptures suggesting that Paul did something that served as the conduit for the attacks that stopped his course. He was just a victim of the coordinated wickedness of the devil against God's plans for his life.

Sometimes someone can be a victim of coordinated attacks of Satan meant to hinder God's will for the person's life. The attacks are not coming as a result of sin, or something, but as a result of the works of the devil. Whatever the case, deliverance is possible in Jesus name.

In the majority of situations, however, there may be something the demons are holding on to. Having a balanced assessment while praying and seeking deliverance is very important. As the wise man said, *"Like a flitting sparrow, like a flying swallow, so a curse without cause shall not alight."* - Proverbs 26:2

A demonic attack will not happen without something empowering it somehow. Be bold enough to discuss and remove anything that might be a link to demonic attacks and evil occurrences in your life and family. If they are specific sins, confess them and repent. If they are habits and attitude issues, surrender them to God and prayerfully begin to change. If they are relationships and soul ties, break free from them and re-commit your life to Christ. If they are materials and objects, ask for wisdom and deal with them. If they are anger, unforgiveness, and bitterness, receive grace to make amends.

The Bible says:

> *Many who had believed now came forward, confessing and disclosing their deeds. And a number of those who had practiced magic arts brought their books and burned them in front of everyone. When the value of the books was calculated, it came to fifty thousand drachmas. So the word of the Lord powerfully continued to spread and prevail* - **Acts 19:18-20**

Deliverance comes through reflection to identify the causes of what's happening and depending on God for help in dealing with these things. So take some time for reflection and praying a prayer of inquiry. Once you're able to discern the sources of the problems, you're halfway solving them. Sometimes this may take days, weeks, months, etc., a lot of time, but it's worth it

Always remember, *"The cause must be dealt with for the curse to be broken."*

And where you're not able to completely figure out some of the causes of the problems in your life or family, trust the Lord as you pray with an open heart. He will intervene in your life.

PRAYERS

Dear Heavenly Father, I pray that You open thou my eyes that I may behold wondrous things out of Thy Law. As I read or listen to Your Word, enlighten my heart, and give me specific leadings for my freedom, healing, restoration, and breakthrough, in Jesus name.

Cause me, O Lord, to hear Your voice telling me the way to pray, the way to go, and the way to respond to the situations in my life today, so that I may experience Your supernatural touch and blessings in every area of my life, in Jesus name

Deliverance by Fire

Father, Your Word says that the Holy Spirit will reveal to us things to come, He will teach us all things, and even bring to our remembrance what You have told us in the past. I pray today, Lord, through the Holy Spirit, teach me all that I need to know and do, even as I wait on You, to be entirely free of the curses and spells working against my life and family before now, in Jesus name.

O Lord, show me everything I need to deal with in my life right now for my deliverance to take effect.

Show me relationships I need to exit. Show me items in my possession that are not of You, that I need to do away with. Show me specific sins, attitudes, and deeds in my life that the devil is using as a leeway into my life, and help me, Lord, to deal with them as You want.

And, Lord, Give me new ideas that will establish Your plan for my life, bring glory to your name, and joy to Your people on earth, in Jesus name.

Lord, according to Jeremiah 33:3, You said that we should call on You in prayer and that You will answer and show us great and mighty things that we do not know.

Many times when David enquired of You regarding a situation, You showed up and gave him clarity. You revealed to him exactly what to do. He would follow Your leading, and You would give Him the victory.

Lord, You have not changed, for You are the same yesterday, today and forever. So I trust You completely to guide me in this situation to victory and breakthrough, and Your name will be glorified, in Jesus name.

Father Lord, if there are specific instructions and direction You gave me in the past which I disregarded, I ask You to forgive me, and set me free from the consequences of disobedience, in the name of Jesus Christ.

Lord, according to Your Word, a curse causeless shall not come. I know there is always something that a problem, an evil, or a situation, will hold as an open door to thrive. So I pray today, Lord, give me insight, revelation, and spiritual understanding so that I can confront the situations I am praying about now from their roots, in Jesus name.

O Lord, unlock my spiritual eyes, ears, and senses today, and open the gate of my heart for Your direction, in the Mighty name of Jesus Christ.

May I no longer grope in darkness. May I no longer be blind spiritually. When I lie down to sleep, Lord, may my dreams be avenues for God's voice. And may I receive divine illumination concerning my life and destiny, in Jesus name.

Amen.

FOR FURTHER READING

Joshua 7, Acts 19

Day 4: How to Obtain Deliverance

"Shake yourself from the dust. Arise and sit down, O Jerusalem. Loose yourself from the yokes of your neck, O captive daughter of Zion." – Isaiah. 52:2.

Anyone who desires deliverance can obtain deliverance when they pray. This is because we hold the key to our lives. The Bible says: *"Deliver thyself as a roe from the hand of the hunter, and as a bird from the hand of the fowler"* - Proverbs 6:5

As the Bible says, you can deliver yourself. You don't need to run to and fro looking for someone to pray over you. Pick your Bible and come before God seeking His intervention in whatever it is that is going wrong in your life at the moment, He will hear you, and help you.

Here are things you need to know and follow through as you seek deliverance.

1. Total Repentance

The Lord is not slack regarding His promise, as some count slackness, but is longsuffering toward us, not willing that any should perish but that all should come to repentance. - 2 Peter 3:9

As a minister, I've seen hundreds of people embark on prayers for deliverance, and nothing happens at the end. I've seen people organize tens and tens of family deliverance prayers; they spend a lot of money, invite men of God to their homes for prayers, but after that, nothing happens.

They buy anointing oils, carry anointed sands, and apply holy waters, yet nothing. Before you know it, they're looking for another prophet or man of God to pray for them again. After months and months of believing that this new prophet's prayers will change things, they see no changes. Then they go searching for another man of God for prayers again. And on and on, the circle continues.

Friend, there's no shortcut to deliverance. You can't buy it with money. You can't earn it by investing and sowing seeds to support the work of God. You only obtain it by the Blood of Jesus Christ. You receive it by repenting from your sins and committing your life to Christ.

For example, you cannot be living a life of immorality, having sex randomly and be praying for deliverance. It will not work. Stop giving excuses and justifying yourself. Take responsibility, repent and ask God for mercy.

God promises to deliver us from all oppressions of the devil, I mean, all of them – whether they be curses, sicknesses, financial lack, marriage problems, infertility, and so on. He can keep His promises to you. However, the first step to real and lasting deliverance and freedom is individual repentance and accepting Jesus Christ as Lord and Savior. You can't use someone else's repentance for your own freedom. No. God doesn't work that way. You must repent and accept Him. Then you can demand your deliverance.

> People want deliverance, they want change, and they search for it desperately, but they don't want to repent of their sins. Too bad. *They want what only God can give, but don't want to take how God wants to give it.*

I'm not talking about going to church. No. Many people go to church but don't know God. You can be going to church but not living for God. You can be going to church but not born again. So what I'm saying is repenting from your sins and cooperating with the Holy Spirit to live a holy life unto the Lord.

What many people are doing today is coming to God and saying: *"Lord, please I need deliverance, here's some money for it. Take this money and give me relief. I'm very busy right now, so I can't give you my life. I've got other things to do with it."*

Unfortunately, it's not working. And it will never work that way.

If you need deliverance, come to God in humility, accept Jesus Christ as your Lord and personal savior, repent of your sins and begin to live for God. That's the first step to deliverance.

2. Fasting and Prayer

Many difficult problems and situations in the Bible were addressed with 'FASTED' PRAYER. Jesus said that some demonic issues can only be fixed by fasting and prayer (Matthew 17:21). Fasting is a very powerful factor in the deliverance process. The Bible says:

"Is not this the kind of fasting I have chosen: to loose the chains of injustice and untie the cords of the yoke, to set the oppressed free and break every yoke? **– Isaiah 58:6**

Fasting will also increase your spiritual sensitivity to perceive what God will be leading you to do. *While the believers were fasting and praying, the Holy Spirit spoke* (Acts 13:2-3). As you fast and pray, pay attention to the leading of the Holy Spirit in your heart. Also, pay attention to your dreams. Whatever the Lord inspires you to deal with, ask for His grace and deal with it.

4. Pray Until You're Free

From my experience, deliverance from some situations is not one day stuff. The demons behind these situations can be very stubborn. So you have to persist in prayers until you are sure it's done.

As I said, no man gives deliverance. Only God gives it. So your deliverance is not in the hand of a man, but God. Don't think that by running from one man of God to the other, it will hasten your deliverance. No. You have to sit down and press for your deliverance with a stubborn faith that refuses nothing else until you're free. Just like the woman in Luke chapter 18, you have to push hard for justice until justice is done.

Usually, when you've obtained deliverance, you'll know. The problem will stop, or you'll have an inner assurance that, yes, the situation is now under control.

> *Until you obtain total deliverance and victory, with practical proof, don't stop praying.*

You should spend time seeking the Lord and praying targeted prayers until God's power is revealed in your life. Where necessary, you may seek prayer support, but the deliverance you do not give yourself first will not come from elsewhere. One thing is sure, as you sincerely and genuinely seek the Lord, He will set you free.

5. Be Sensitive as You Pray

As you pray and seek the Lord for deliverance from the wicked works of the devil, you will have revelations a couple of times, either in dreams, trances, serious impressions or insights while reading the bible. These may contain essential instructions you need to carry out. When you have such insights or revelations, write them down. And quickly set about doing them.

Usually, when you're seeking deliverance, your dreams will be a pointer to whether you have obtained deliverance or not. If you regularly have dreams of victory, peace, and breakthrough, then you've broken the chains. But when your dreams are constant attacks, you have to keep pushing in prayers. Your dreams and other spiritual revelations contain keys to your prayers.

6. Know and Use the Best Hours to Pray

What are the best times to pray for deliverance?

The three daily special times of prayer recorded in both the Old and New Testaments were explicitly the third hour, the sixth hour and the ninth hour of the day, or 9:00 A.M., 12 noon and 3:00 P.M. The Apostles observed them in the New Testament. However, they were not a part of the Law of Moses or Jesus Christ, and nowhere in the Bible is their compliance mandatory.

With the liberty we have in Christ, these times may be easily adapted or adjusted to fit your contemporary daily schedule. I have slightly modified these prayer times based on what works more effectively in deliverance experiences and scriptural insights. So here are the times we recommend that you select from and pray for your deliverance:

- 12:00 midnight - 1:00am (Midnight Period)
- 3:00 am – 4:00 am (Early Morning Period)
- 6:00am – 7:00am (Morning Period)
- 9:00 A.M. – 10:00 A.M – Third Hour Session
- 12:00 – 1:00 pm (Midday or Sixth Hour Session)
- 3:00 pm – 4:00 pm (Afternoon or Ninth hour Session)

<u>Deliverance by Fire</u>

- 9:00pm – 10:00pm (Night Session)

You may choose any of these sessions and pray. There are no laws, which means you could chose afternoon session today and pray, and chose night session tomorrow and pray. Whatever is convenient for your schedule is welcome.

However, we always recommend the midnight and early morning sessions. For some mysterious reasons, the night hours provides a better atmosphere for earnest warfare prayers. And yes, what happens in the night can drastically influence the results of the day. The Bible says:

> You will not be afraid of the terror of night, nor the arrow that flies by day - **Psalm 91:5**
>
> But while men slept, his enemy came and sowed tares among the wheat, and went his way. - **Matthew 13:25**
>
> Everyone who does evil hates the day, and will not come into the light for fear that their deeds will be exposed - **John 3:30**.
>
> Do not desire the night, when people are cut off in their place. - **Job 36:20**

All these scriptures are explicitly saying that the night hours has strong spiritual significance to our lives.

David said in Psalm 119:62, *"At midnight I will rise to give thanks to You, because of Your righteous judgments."* As a prophet, he knew the power of midnight prayers. As he prayed in those times, he saw God's righteous judgments on his enemies. You'll want to do the same thing if you desire quick judgments on all your oppression.

The Bible says in Exodus 12:29 that *"at midnight the LORD smote all the firstborn in the land of Egypt, from the firstborn of Pharaoh that sat on his throne unto the firstborn of the captive that was in the dungeon; and all the firstborn of cattle."* At midnight Paul and Silas prayed and sang praise unto the Lord, and an angel freed them (Acts 16:25).

Use the midnight hours, like Samson did, to uproot the gates of your enemy. Prayers to dislodge evil powers, obtain deliverance, and break demonic covenants are best done in the night hours, especially from Midnight to 6:00 A.M. Praying at these times gives you the needed concentration and focus to destroy whatever the enemies have disseminated, and release your stolen blessings.

PRAYERS

O Lord my Father, I declare today that I am ready for my deliverance. I am ready to be free from all forms of limitations in my life, in Jesus name.

Lord, I shake myself from the dust from this day forward; I arise and **loose myself from the bands of my neck. I declare my captivity no more, in Jesus name.**

As I begin to pray, Lord, empower me with great passion and determination to persist in prayers until the manifestation of my deliverance and breakthrough.

I will not take no for an answer. I will not give up and accept any evil harassment in my life and family as normal. Never. Jesus Christ came that I might have life and have it abundantly. That is what will happen to me, in Jesus name.

Father, Lord, as I pray today, I confess my sins and recommit my life to the Lord Jesus Christ.

There are many times I let my desires, judgments, and human perceptions prevail in my relationship with You and others. There are many times I let my flesh decide for me what to do and how to live.

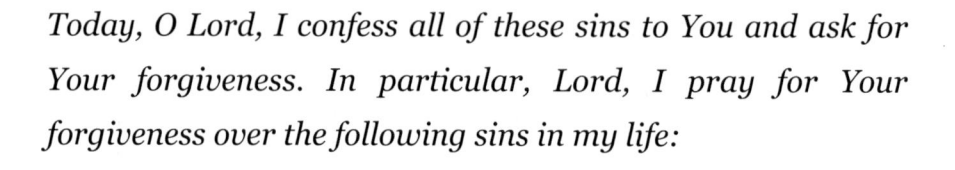

Today, O Lord, I confess all of these sins to You and ask for Your forgiveness. In particular, Lord, I pray for Your forgiveness over the following sins in my life:

....

(Mention specific areas of your life that need to be brought open before the Lord)

Father, I am sorry for letting these sins rule my life. I confess them before Thee today and accept Your gift of forgiveness. Please give me the grace to overcome these sins and live for Thy glory from now onwards, in Jesus name.

Lord, I ask Thee for grace to forgive those who have sinned against me from the past through to this moment. I surrender to You any bitterness in my heart and ask for Your healing and restoration. I release all of the hurts and pains in my heart to You today and plead the Blood of Jesus Christ in my spirit, soul, and body.

I declare today that I completely forgive all those who have offended me; I release them from the captivity of bitterness in my heart.

Deliverance by Fire

Through the Blood and name of Jesus Christ, I reclaim every benefit, opportunity, and blessing that unforgiveness has delayed or denied in my life, in Jesus name.

O Lord, please touch the heart of those I have offended to forgive and forget my offenses. Give us the opportunity to amend our ways and follow after peace once again.

Father, if there are people I need to forgive for my life to breakthrough, please lead me to them now in Jesus name.

Dear Fire of the Holy Spirit, purge my heart of every unforgiveness, bitterness, regret, self-pity, low self-esteem, dwelling on the past, and vengeance thoughts, in Jesus name.

Lord, as I wait on you this period, remove from me every form of distraction. Empower me with the strength to be focused and hear how You are leading me to pray and what You are leading me to do. And baptize me with an unusual spiritual sensitivity to discern Your direction in prayer, in Jesus name.

Amen.

FURTHER READING

Joel 2 and Acts 2

Day 5: Understanding Our Tools for Deliverance

10 Finally, my brethren, be strong in the Lord and in the power of His might. 11 Put on the whole armor of God, that you may be able to stand against the wiles of the devil. 12 For we do not wrestle against flesh and blood, but against principalities, against powers, against the rulers of the darkness of this age, against spiritual hosts of wickedness in the heavenly places.

13 Therefore take up the whole armor of God, that you may be able to withstand in the evil day, and having done all, to stand.

14 Stand therefore, having girded your waist with truth, having put on the breastplate of righteousness, 15 and having shod your feet with the preparation of the gospel of peace; 16 above all, taking the shield of faith with which you will be able to quench all the fiery darts of the wicked one. 17 And take the helmet of salvation, and the sword of the Spirit, which is the word of God. – **Eph. 6:10-14**

In this scripture, Apostle Paul uses imagery of a typical Roman soldier of his day to teach believers their weapons of warfare. While the Roman soldier is fighting physical battles, the believer is engaged in a more tough fight – spiritual wars. Hence the believer needs to be sure he is adequately equipped.

There is a severe spiritual fight going on against your marriage, health, family, children, and ministry. You don't leave this battle up to God and say, *"Well, I can't do anything. Let the will of God be done."*

If there's nothing we can do Paul wouldn't bother telling us to wear our weapons of warfare. Who dresses for war and then sits down to play around? There would be no need to instruct people to dress for battle if there was no war going on. It's as simple as ABC.

There is a spiritual war going on against you. That's why you're instructed to *wear the belt of truth, the breastplate of righteousness, the shoe of the gospel of peace, the shield of faith, the helmet of salvation, and the sword of the Spirit, which is the word of God.*

Let's look at various instruments that God has provided for our deliverance, in addition to these weapons that the Apostle Paul talked about. These are specific tools and instruments we must know, trust and apply as we pray for deliverance from anything.

1. The Name of Jesus Christ

In the name of Jesus Christ, is not just an enchanted incantation that is appended on to the end of prayers. **The name of Jesus Christ**, is an acknowledgment of our position in Christ and an understanding that God hears our prayers as we approach His throne of grace.

Praying in Jesus name means praying according to God's will.

*Philippians 2:8-11 - 8 And being found in appearance as a man, He humbled Himself and became obedient to the point of death, even the death of the cross. 9 Therefore God also has highly exalted Him and given Him the name which is above every name, 10 that **at the name of Jesus every knee should bow**, of those in heaven, and of those on earth, and of those under the earth, 11 and that every tongue should confess that Jesus Christ is Lord, to the glory of God the Father.*

Mark 16:17-18 - And these signs will follow those who believe: In My name they will cast out demons; they will speak with new tongues; they will take up serpents; and if they drink anything deadly, it will by no means hurt them; they will lay hands on the sick, and they will recover.

Acts 4:11-12 - This is the 'stone which was rejected by you builders, which has become the chief cornerstone.' Nor is there salvation in any other, for there is no other name under heaven given among men by which we must be saved.

2. The Blood of Jesus Christ

The Blood of Jesus Christ is another powerful instrument of our deliverance. "Of all the wonderful things that the blood means," says Andrew Murray, "… His blood is the sign, the degree, yes, the impartation of His love." As a reminder, here are things that the Blood of Jesus Christ has done for us:

=> ***We have total redemption*** *through the Blood of Jesus* (Ephesians 1:7): The Blood washed our sins away and set us free from the curse of the law (death, sin, sickness, disease, poverty, lack, depression—anything bad you can think of) so that we may inherit the Blessing of Abraham.

=> ***We have unrestricted access*** *to God through the Blood* (Hebrews 10:19): Because of the blood of Jesus, you can come boldly into the presence of God and have fellowship with Him.

=> ***We are healed*** *through the Blood of Jesus* (Isaiah 53:5): the Blood is also our ticket to healing. If the devil tries to mess up with your mind or your health, remember the Blood of Jesus Christ.

=> **The Blood of Jesus protects** us from evil (Exodus 12:13): When Pharaoh stubbornly refused to let the Israelites go, God sent a final plague—one of judgment—to smite all the firstborn in the land of Egypt. God told them to take the blood of a lamb and paint it on their doorposts. This was a symbol of the blood of the Jesus who was slain from the foundation of the world (Revelation 13:8). They did, and the messenger of death passed them by. As we apply the blood of Jesus over our family and household from time to time, we can be sure that the Blood will protect us.

=> **We overcome the devil** through the Blood of Jesus (Rev. 12:11): As believers in Christ, we have authority over Satan. By pleading the blood of Jesus Christ in prayers – every day – we exercise that authority and take back what the enemy has stolen from us.

The Blood of Jesus Christ is a powerful instrument for our deliverance. As we pray and plead the Blood of Jesus Christ we invoke God's power to do all the far-reaching things His Word says He wants to do.

By believing in the gift and power of the Blood of Jesus Christ and praying with it, we will see relationships healed, physical needs provided, finances restored, protection received, supernatural intervention occur, and many other things happen. God will always answer the Blood of Jesus Christ.

3. The Power of the Holy Communion

As for you also, by the blood of thy covenant, I have sent forth your prisoners out of the pit where there is no water (Zechariah 9:11)

The Blood of Jesus Christ is the seal of the new covenant. Under it, there's nothing hidden that will not be made known. His Blood invokes our deliverance and establishes us in God's presence.

While praying for deliverance, one way to spiritually disconnect yourself from all forms of evil covenants, evil activities and establish your union in the covenant of the Blood of Jesus Christ is continually using the symbol of the Holy Communion.

> Then Jesus said to them, 'Most assuredly, I say to you, unless you eat the flesh of the Son of Man and drink His blood, you have no life in you.' - **John 6:53**
>
> For as often as ye eat this bread, and drink this cup, ye do shew the Lord's death till he come. - **1 Cor. 11:26**.

Apart from waiting to take the Holy Communion in Church service, you can prepare this spiritual meal and use it to minister deliverance and healing to yourself. Yes, you can take the Holy Communion personally as a way to spiritualize your unity and connection to Christ's death and resurrection. And use the exercise to claim your translation from the kingdom of darkness to the kingdom of light, claim your healing, physical body restoration, and deliverance from all forms of evil harassments against your life and family.

I encourage you to prepare the communion and take it every night after your prayers and use it to declare your freedom in Christ.

4. The Power of Declaring Scriptures

. 17And take the helmet of salvation, and the sword of the Spirit, which is the word of God.

The Word of God is described as the sword of the spirit. I'm sure if Apostle Paul were writing today, he would replace the word **sword** there with something like a *gun*, *bomb*, or something more fitting in modern warfare. As the sword is used for slaying the enemies, guns are used to shoot down targets.

The Word of God is our guns in prayer and spiritual warfare. When we release them, we send unstoppable bullets against the enemy, slay them, and obtain victory where necessary.

Don't just pray for praying sake. Read the Word of God, meditate on it, and then pray them over the situations you need deliverance from.

When Christ was confronted by Satan after His 40 days and nights fasting, He prayed the Word of God, and not human Words. Three times He said: ***"It is written…"*** The devil tried to persist, but gave up finally and ran away.

That's the template for overcoming the devil and obtaining deliverance in any area that he attacks us. If our health is attacked, we find scriptures and God's promises regarding our health and continue to meditate and pray them until our total restoration. If our finances are attacked, we locate scriptures and promises on our finances and pray them until our blessings show forth. The same thing applies to further areas of life.

Praying scriptures is the most powerful way to pray. *For the word of God is living and powerful, and sharper than any two-edged sword, piercing even to the division of soul and spirit, and of joints and marrow, and is a discerner of the thoughts and intents of the heart* (Hebrews 4:12).

In Genesis 31:3, God made a promise to Jacob, saying, "*I will be with you.*" That is, "*I will deal well with you.*" Then later, when in terrible crises, Jacob cries out to God in prayer and reminds Him of his promise to him. He says: "*O God of my father Abraham, and God of my father Isaac,* **the Lord which saidst unto me, Return unto thy country, and to thy kindred, and I will deal well with thee**... (Genesis 32:9-12)

He reminded God of His promises. He prayed the Word of God.

The fuel of prayer is the Word of God. We remind God in our prayer what He has said and call Him to be faithful to His Word. That is the very backbone of all faith-filled praying. *"For all the promises of God in him are yea, and in him Amen, unto the glory of God by us."* - 2 Corinthians 1:20

5. The Weapon of Faith

Above all, taking the shield of faith with which you will be able to quench all the fiery darts of the wicked one (Eph. 6:14).

Faith is also a potent force in our spiritual warfare. That is why Paul said, *"Above all, take the shield of faith."* Without faith we may pray and never obtain victory. As the scripture says, without faith we cannot please God.

Why is faith a weapon that we must, "above all, take?"

A shield is critical to a soldier. It offers a blanket of protection. Such armor was not just self-protective but could also be used to push back adversaries. So it's is meant to be taken up in all situations. It is the first barricade against the enemy's attack. Today, a shield would represent a bulletproof vest in military warfare. Without this vest, one can easily get killed by an enemy's shot.

So why must we take the weapon of faith as we pray for deliverance?

The answer is simple. Without faith, the enemy will hurt you.

You can pray all the prayers in this world, but if you don't believe in your prayers, if you don't believe that God is at work in your life, if you don't believe that what you're praying and commanding will happen, you'll fall back to actions and words that cancel your prayers from time to time.

6. The Weapon of Fire

As I said earlier, fire is an instrument of judgment against the works of the wicked. As Elijah called down fire to judge the prophets of Baal, we can call down fire to judge negative threats that rise against our lives and family from time to time.

Fire has no respect for faces. Fire does not beg. Fire consumes. When fire attacks, you better stay off the way. When we pray, we can call down fire to judge the wicked and release our blessings.

6. The Power of the Anointing Oil

Is anyone sick among you? Let him call for the elders of the church, and let them pray over him, anointing him with oil in the name of the Lord. And a prayer of faith will save the sick, and the Lord will raise him up. And if he has committed sins, he will be forgiven. – **James 5:14-15**

One night as we were all asleep, our one-year-old daughter, Annabel, suddenly started crying. She cried and cried and would not stop. We did everything physically possible to stop her from crying, but she did not. We wanted to rush her to the hospital, but it was in the middle of the night, so couldn't do much. So my wife and I decided to pray over her. We somehow felt she must have had a spiritual attack in the dream or so. Yes, children can also be attacked by the devil. They can also have nightmares and other spiritual issues that only prayer and counseling can resolve.

So we decided to pray for her. We prayed a prayer of agreement using a few scriptures that we always use to pray for children. After the agreement prayer with my wife, I carried her and asked my wife to go back to bed. I took her to the sitting room and began to anoint her and speak God's WORD over her life. Twenty minutes later, she stopped crying and slept off in my arms.

We may not know exactly what happened that night as she was just one-year-old and may never explain to us. But we obtained victory in the name of Jesus Christ, using spiritual tools the Lord has instructed us to use – a prayer of agreement and the anointing oil.

Ministering to ourselves with anointing oil is something we should all learn to do from time to time. The anointing oil is a symbol of the Holy Spirit used for consecration, healing, and enthronement.

During your prayer rounds for deliverance, always anoint yourself after a prayer session, and declare yourself dedicated and consecrated to the Lord. As a dedicated instrument to God, no demon has right over your life anymore.

PRAYERS

Heavenly Father, I thank You for the gift of the name of Jesus Christ. Thank You for the gift and work of the Blood of Jesus

Christ. Thank You for the power available to us through the Holy Communion, the anointing oil, the Scriptures, faith and Your fire.

Indeed, Lord, You have given us everything we need for our freedom and deliverance. Be glorified forever and ever in Jesus name.

Thank You, Lord, for giving me boldness to come before Your throne of Grace to obtain help in time of need, through the Blood of Jesus Christ. I am not helpless, Lord, for You are my ever present help.

There is no more condemnation on me for the Blood of Jesus Christ is speaking on my behalf continually. For this I say, thank You, Lord, in Jesus name.

Today, O Lord, I put on the whole armor of God. I stand against the wiles of the enemy in my life and family.

I declare them destroyed forever and ever, in Jesus name.

I gird my waist today with the truth of God's infallible Word. I lay on the breastplate of righteousness and shod my feet with the gospel of peace.

I take the shield of faith and begin to quench all the fiery darts of the wicked one.

I take the helmet of the assurance of my salvation in Christ, and attack, with the sword of the Spirit - which is the word of God - all agents of darkness carrying out evil against my life and family. I command them exposed, frustrated and exiled today, in Jesus name.

I call upon You Lord to baptize me with fresh fire from heaven. Reconnect me to the depth of Your Love and holiness. May I be consecrated to Thee O Lord, in Jesus name.

I charge myself in the fire of the Holy Spirit today, and take authority in the name of Jesus Christ over every evil decrees against my life, against my marriage, against my family, and against my ministry. I decree today that I and my family are saved, in the name of the LORD, in Jesus name. Amen.

FOR FURTHER READING

Ephesians 6 and 2 Corinthians 10

Day 6: Dealing With Satanic Strongholds

₄For the weapons of our warfare are not carnal but mighty in God to pull down of strongholds, ₅casting down arguments and every high thing that exalts itself against the knowledge of God, bringing every thought into captivity to the obedience of Christ, ₆ and being ready to punish all disobedience when your obedience is fulfilled.- **2 Corinthians 10:4-6**

Strongholds are lies that we have accepted as truths. I call them Satan's propaganda that we unconsciously accept and hold against God's Words. Unfortunately, they are just lies that have been repeatedly told to us over and over, such that we now vigorously defend them unknowingly.

In today's reading, Paul describes strongholds as arguments, pretensions, or thoughts that set themselves contrary to the knowledge of God. Any principles, theories, views or beliefs ingrained in our thinking that are different to the truth as written in Scripture are strongholds of the Enemy that stand in the way of our knowing God and making Him known. Thus they draw us back in our walk with the Lord and our prayer and worship lives.

Here are a few examples of strongholds:

- I will never get out of debt
- I will never be free from this addiction
- I am no good; I am worthless
- I won't find love after all
- My husband is hopeless. He'll never be saved.
- I'm just a fleshy person. I'll never be free from lust.
- I'll always struggle to make ends meet.
- I always have this sickness. It's a part of me.
- I'll probably never get married

Each of these arguments reflects interpretations rooted in the mind that are contrary to God's will as revealed in Scripture. These deceptions which form mental strongholds can come from a wide range of sources, including our environment, failed relationships, friendships, parents, news, medical diagnosis, experiences of failure and pain in the past, or demons. Letting these lies control us can lead to living a defeated life.

Strongholds can also be physical. Physical strongholds are negative habits and attitudes in us that are continually struggling with our knowing God. The more we struggle with these habits, the more the enemy builds further limitations against our lives. For instance, you may be praying to lose weight, while you're still tied to overeating. In this instance, overeating becomes a stronghold fighting against God's health plan for your life.

You may be praying for financial deliverance and breakthrough while you're still tied to impulse buying, ignoring your bills, careless spending, always expecting financial miracles instead of looking for work, and spending more than you earn. In this case, your negative financial habits are strongholds that must be dealt with for you to experience God's financial breakthrough.

Today, we're going to take time to speak into our lives and command every mental or physical stronghold that gives the devil a leeway to build a blockade over our lives and destiny to be destroyed. We are going to receive total empowerment to break free from these mental deceptions and habits that are inimical to our spiritual and physical progress.

There are three ways to deal with strongholds. They are:

- Identify the strongholds

- Attack the strongholds

- Believe and declare your victory every day.

IDENTIFYING STRONGHOLDS

Mark Virkler, founder, and president of Christian Leadership University listed over ten groups of strongholds that the enemy could use to bind us. They are:

Group 1: Fear related strongholds

The Fear of man, the fear of what people will say, fear of criticism, doubt/unbelief, fright, worry, anxiety, always fearing the worst will happen, fear of various illnesses like cancer, fear people will get angry with you or won't like you, spirit of false responsibility, always in a rush

Group 2: Anger related strongholds

Hatred, malice, rage, murder thoughts, uncontrollable temper, always cursing, vengeance and retaliatory tendencies, violence, abuse, cruelty, sadism, unforgiveness, bitterness, being judgmental or too critical, always easily taking offense, easily feeling irritated, unfounded anger towards men or women, unforgettable anger towards mother or father, anger and resentment towards God.

Group 3: Addictions related strongholds

Addictions to alcohol, tobacco, drugs, food, sugar, coffee, chocolate/sweets, pornography, sex, flirtation, horror/vampire movies, TV, etc.

Group 4: False judgmental strongholds

Always feeling abandoned, rejected, neglected, lonely, isolated, self-pity, self-condemnation, self-victimization, unable to value people and relationships, always quickly ending relationships, and burning bridges, disgrace, embarrassment, guilt, hatred for life, self-hate, withdrawal, hiding/antisocial, timidity, inferiority, etc.

Group 5: Deceit related strongholds

Always lying, cheating, stealing, deceitful, fraudulent, untrustworthy, adulterous, overly secretive, hiding purchases, activities and relationships

Group 6: Sensual related strongholds

Lust, fantasizing and coveting another's mate, flirtatious living, addiction to sex outside marriage, sexual abuse, rape, incest, pornography, emotional adultery.

Group 7: Depression-related strongholds

Feeling rejected, dejected and despondent, feeling helpless, hopeless, constant sadness, self-pity, withdrawal, suicide thoughts, mood swings, constant moving from low to high moments, persistent grief, sorrow, loss, pain, torment, weeping, anguish, agony, etc.

Group 8: Narcissistic related strongholds

Pride, arrogance, disdain, selfishness, control/pushiness, callousness/lack of concern for others, excessive interest in or admiration of oneself, gossip, etc.

Group 9: A "want mentality" stronghold

Belief in poverty, not believing in covenant blessings, always in debt, always in lack, never taking responsibility for failure, greedy for other's benefits, dishonest in money matters, idolization of possessions, etc.

Group 10: Inaction related strongholds

Constant procrastination, slothfulness, laziness, distracted and confused living, lack of focus, lack of organization, in a haste to do things without preparation, continuous lateness and tardiness, always missing appointments, phone calls, and schedules.

Group 11: Mental instability strongholds

Mental illness, compulsions, confusion, hysteria, paranoia, schizophrenia, insanity, panics, over critical of others, feeling too competitive, etc.

ATTACKING THE STRONGHOLDS

The list of strongholds above sounds like a lot of stuff to deal with. Sure. But remember that these strongholds can hinder our prayers. They can bind us and prevent our deliverance from whatever it is we are praying for. So, it's time to deal with these strongholds.

If you identify any of these strongholds as something you're struggling with, be honest with yourself and acknowledge your need for divine help. Remember, *"He who covers his sins will not prosper, but whoever confesses and forsakes them will have mercy"* (Proverbs 28:13).

As we present these strongholds to the Lord in prayer, expect deliverance in the name of Jesus Christ. And expect divine empowerment to walk in daily victory.

DECLARE YOUR VICTORY EVERY DAY

Just so you know, the enemy can come back over and over to try to rebuild a stronghold. So be aware that after praying against these strongholds, they may try to raise their ugly heads again. But you don't have to be bound to them. You must continually use the Word of God to speak to these mental and physical strongholds, refusing to accept their verdicts about you. As you continue to **bring every thought into captivity to the obedience of Christ,** they will stop harassing your walk with God.

PRAYERS

Father in heaven, by Your mercies, I come to present my life, my thoughts and my body to You as a living sacrifice. Make me holy and acceptable to Your service, in Jesus name.

O Lord, I hand over my thoughts and dedicate my mind, imaginations, and attitudes unto You. I ask that You uproot out of my life every inner argument, every emotional disagreement, and unbelief contesting Your Word in my life.

I arrest all negative thought, in me, resisting the move of the Holy Spirit. I command these thoughts to wither by fire in the name of Jesus Christ.

Father, I present these strongholds to You today. I bring them under Thy feet that I may find mercy and help for freedom from these binding issues. O Lord, here are the strongholds that I see in my life

....

Mention specific strongholds in your life that needs to leave

Father, deliver me from these strongholds, in Jesus name.

Today, O Lord, I speak to all of these spiritual strongholds in my life working against the knowledge of God. I command them to die by fire, in the name of Jesus Christ.

May every false god contesting for worship in my life cease to exist today, in Jesus name.

Every Idol in my life challenging Lordship with You, Lord Jesus Christ, I overthrow them today by fire in the name of Jesus.

---

*I command the idols of mammon, greed, lust, pornography, anger, bitterness (**mention other idols**) over my life to die by fire today in the name of Jesus Christ.*

By the priceless Blood of Jesus Christ, I severe myself from every mental stronghold binding me to the devil and limiting the blessings of God in my life. I declare my thoughts, imaginations, brain, and meditations sanctified by the Blood of Jesus Christ, in Jesus name.

I speak to every physical stronghold of bad habit in my life to end today, in the name of Jesus.

I squeeze the life out of the powers responsible for these negative habits in my life. I command them to seize to exist. And I claim my freedom in Jesus name.

You demons pushing me to sin and live against the knowledge and will of God for my life, I bind you all today and send you all into the abyss. Remain there and come back no more into my life in Jesus name.

No demon has a legal right over my life anymore, for my life is hid in Christ and Christ in God. The life I live now is not mine, but Christ's. So I declare that I will live every day of my life for the Glory of God, in Jesus name.

I command fire from heaven to destroy every root of sin and ungodly habit in my life, causing a barrier between me and the power of God, in Jesus name.

O Lord, plant in me an everlasting hatred for lust, anger, bitterness, alcoholism, smoking, overeating (gluttony), and any other detrimental lifestyle hitherto warring against me and frustrating my spiritual growth, in Jesus name.

O Lord, may whatever evil consequence in my life, resulting from my attitude, past mistakes, or addictions to negative thoughts, words, and habits, seize today. Whatever curses and obstacles that my wrong thoughts, words, behaviors, associations, and friendships have brought upon my life, let them be destroyed today in the name of Jesus Christ.

Precious Holy Spirit, I call on You today to empower me to bear Your fruits in my life every day. Help me to walk in **Love, Peace, Joy, Patience, Gentleness, Kindness and Self-Control,** *in Jesus name.*

O Lord, surround me with the right people – surround me with people who will challenge me towards a Godly and excellent life – from today.

I commit myself never to walk in the counsel of the ungodly, nor stand in the way of sinners, nor dine with mockers. I commit myself to delight in the Word of God and fellowship.

I shall henceforth depend on God's Word day and night, and its power shall work in me, always, to bear the right fruits.

For I am like a tree planted by the side of the river. My strength shall not fail. From season to season I shall bear fruit… in Jesus Mighty name.

Amen.

FOR FURTHER READING

Read Judges 16 and pray that God will give you victory over the Philistines (strongholds). But pray that you will not die with these strongholds

Day 7: Dealing With Negative Soul Ties, Agreements and Vows

Culled from my book, Breaking Soul Ties

Be not unequally yoked together with unbelievers: for what fellowship hath righteousness with unrighteousness? And what communion hath light with darkness? - **2 Corinthians 6:14**

Deliverance is an inside job. Most times we're consumed with wanting the outside circumstances to change that we don't look inside enough to deal with issues that can be responsible for what we're going through. One such often ignored question capable of being a serious source of spiritual problems is negative soul ties and agreements.

It is often said that a friendly enemy is more dangerous than a visible enemy. Winston Churchill said, *"When there is no enemy within, the enemies outside cannot hurt you."* Jesus said: *"And a man's foes shall be they of his household"* (Matthew 10:36).

That is how soul ties, negative agreements, and vows are. They can be a reason why someone is suffering while the person is busy looking for outside demons and enemies.

It is possible for someone to come under demonic attacks and oppression as a result of unholy agreements, covenants, soul-ties or relationships. So let's look into breaking these unholy agreements, covenants, and bonds that you may have entered into, knowingly or unknowingly, which is now a spiritual barrier to God's plans for your life.

WHAT ARE SOUL TIES?

Soul-ties are affectionate bonding between two souls. Something like an intense, cherished relationship between two or more persons, usually with a goal to work for each other's welfare and protection. It's so unfathomable that each party in the relationship is unconsciously pushed by a force to remain loyal, never complain and to protect the interest of the other party. An example is what happened between David and Jonathan.

> *After David had finished talking with Saul, Jonathan became one in spirit with David, and he loved him as himself.*
> *Then Jonathan and David made a covenant because he loved him as his own soul.* - **1 Sam 18:1, 3**

Jonathan's soul was attracted to David, so much that he gave up a lot for him, including his kingly inheritance. This example worked out the purpose of God, so we'd say it was a positive mind connection.

And yes, when a soul is tied to another soul for positive purposes, it can bring about a great mutually beneficial good. But when one party is on the receiving end, and cannot break free for some unknown reasons, it becomes an unholy soul tie.

There is a case that recently made a national headline a few months back. A man in his 30s secretly abducted a girl of 12-13 years old and continuously used the girl for his sexual gain. She was his sex slave for several months. When the girl was found after an intensive search, she refused to leave her abuser calming that she was in love with him.

Can you imagine that?

That is a clear case of negative soul tie. Whatever words or charms the man used to seduce the girl had gotten into her brain and soul to the extent she couldn't make sound judgments again.

Have you seen someone that is so involved with a person to the extent that even when it is evident that the fellow is just taking advantage of this person, they still find it difficult to leave? That's how a soul tie works. I have had people, especially ladies, come to me to pray for their boyfriends to leave every other woman out there and stick with them. Sometimes when I probe further, I will recognize that these sisters are willing to do anything on earth to be in the lives of these their boyfriends. Some are willing to be abused, slaved, slept with, and maltreated as long as they are together.

One case comes to mind. This sister wrote:

She: *"Pastor, please pray that my boyfriend never leaves me again for another lady. Pray that all the ladies after him be blinded by fire."*

Me: *"Ok, Let's pray. But before we do, can I ask you a few questions?"*

She: *"Yes pastor, go on."*

Me: *Thanks. My first question: are you guys married?"*

She: *"No, pastor."*

Me: *"Are you sleeping with him?"*

She: *"Yes, pastor."*

Me: *"Why are you sleeping with him when you're not married? Don't you know that's a sin and improper? "*

She: *"I'm sorry pastor. But I don't want him to leave me again for another girl."*

Me: *"Okay, has he proposed to you? Are you guys talking about marriage?"*

She: *"No sir, he has not proposed sir. But I know he will marry me. I don't want to rush him. I want to take it easy with him. I love him, and he loves me too. I'm doing everything I can to make sure he's happy."*

Me:?

Many times, soul ties start out as simple love relationships. It gets to a level where one party becomes the supplier of the love and the ingredients of its service. Even when it's evident that they are being abused and hurt, they still can't find the courage to detach from the relationship. And even when forced to leave, they still can't move on wholeheartedly.

Soul ties are usually formed through sexual entanglements before marriage or outside marriage. That's why the Bible warns against sex outside marriage because sex is not just what movies and friends say it is. It is a covenant. It is more spiritual than the physical enjoyment part of it.

Here are signs that one may be under a soul tie:

- You are in an abusive relationship - physically, emotionally or spiritually – and you feel so attached to that person that you refuse to disconnect and set limits.

- You are unable to move on wholeheartedly from a relationship you have left (maybe long ago). You continue to be obsessed with the other person (you can't get them out of your mind).

- You continue to feel that this person is watching or monitoring you in anything you do. You feel that you cannot make a sound judgment without this person.

- When you're having sex with someone else (your marriage partner), you can hardly keep yourself from visualizing this person.

- You find yourself always comparing your present partner with this person. You always feel that your current partner is inferior to this person, and needs to upgrade in some way.

- You may find yourself secretly stalking this person and still wanting to prevent them from having another relationship outside you, even though you're no longer together.

- You find yourself always defending this person; even when it's clear that you are hurt and maltreated, you still feel that this person must be justified.

- In some cases, you may find yourself unknowingly having the same traits, moods and even sicknesses that this person is suffering.

- You have an emotional reaction that is unpleasant when someone mentions their name or if you run into them unexpectedly.

Soul ties can pose a source of spiritual obstacles if not prayerfully dealt with. So look into your life right now and begin to renounce every soul tie that may be working against God's purpose for your life unknowingly.

NEGATIVE AGREEMENTS AND ALLIANCES

Negative agreements can also be a ground for satanic attacks against our lives. These may be just ignorant agreements of, "I will marry you," "You will marry me," agreements that a girl and a boy makes. They may go ahead to say things like, *"If I don't marry you, let this or that happen... I won't amount to anything without you."* They may even go further to seal the agreement with blood or other simple tokens.

The disadvantage of these agreements is that spirits don't forget them. The boy or girl may forget and go on to live their lives, but the spirits that witnessed this **yoking together** will use it as a ground to afflict them so severely until this is discovered and brought to light in prayers.

Another aspect of yoking together that can be a ground for the devil to build restrictions against a person is going into business with someone who has evil spirits and demonic influences, who may be under a spiritual judgment. Remember Jonah. He was under a spiritual punishment for disobedience and almost caused the people he was traveling with to sink until he was fished out.

We are not against business partnership at all. But we advise that before you go into any business alliance with someone, take some time to pray through and be sure you have an inner witness to go ahead with the business relationship.

UNFULFILLED VOWS AND PLEDGES

Unfulfilled vows and pledges can also be a ground for spiritual restrictions against a person. Solomon advised:

> [1] *My son, if you have put up security for your neighbor, if you have shaken hands in pledge for a stranger,* [2] *you have been trapped by what you said, ensnared by the words of your mouth.*
> [3] *So do this, my son, to free yourself since you have fallen into your neighbor's hands:* [4] *Go to the point of exhaustion and give your neighbor no rest! Allow no sleep to your eyes, no slumber to your*

*eyelids. ₅Free yourself, like a gazelle from the hand of the hunter, like a bird from the snare of the fowler. – **Proverbs 6:1-5***

This scripture is very clear. It's possible for you to have made promises and pledges that are now a ground for you to suffer some limitations. If possible, go and unmake these promises and free yourself. That's what the Scripture is saying. These pledges can be borrowings that you did and signed some harsh agreements for.

God is not happy when we make promises that we don't keep. Ecclesiastes 5:5 says that *"It is better not to make a vow than to make one and not fulfill it."*

In the Church, many preachers try to entice people with sweet words and even outright lies and exaggerations to push them to make vows and financial pledges. And a lot of the time, most of these vows are not fulfilled, and we make more and more vows as the days go by.

This is nothing but folly.

Today, if there are vows, pledges and promises you have made here and there; if there are borrowings you have done and entered into all manner of promises and agreements, you need to start working towards redeeming them; and afterward, decide not to be pushed to make pledges and vows unnecessarily. However, if you think you can't keep these promises any longer, then get back to those involved and discuss the situation. I once had to text someone to reduce the amount I had pledged and offered what I could afford.

The Bible says, *"Free yourself, like a gazelle from the hand of the hunter, like a bird from the snare of the fowler."*

That's what we must do.

PRAYERS

1. TO BREAK SOUL TIES

Dear Heavenly Father, I confidently come before your throne of grace, covered in the Blood of Jesus Christ.

I ask You to disconnect me from any evil soul ties between myself and anyone else, created by any relationship, sexual or otherwise, known or unknown, in Jesus name.

From today O LORD, I cut off all ungodly soul ties formed by any relationship. I unyoke myself from every evil yoke and distance myself from every unrighteous relationship, in Jesus name.

Deliverance by Fire

Father, according to YOUR Word, I present my body to You as a living sacrifice, holy and pleasing to YOU. Lord, empower me to offer true and proper worship acceptable to You at all times, in Jesus name.

O LORD, guide my footsteps to take the right path in my life journey.

Empower and guide me through the Holy Spirit to choose friends and relationships that will bring praise to Your Holy name, forever and ever, in Jesus name.

O LORD, as I encounter new individuals daily, my soul may become tangled with another causing me to idolize that individual and to lose sight of Your great plan and purpose for my life. I may even lose who I really am and who You created me to be.

LORD, in those moments of weakness, Let the Holy Spirit wake me up from slumber and remind me strongly who I am in Christ Jesus and help me to measure all friendships and relationships according to Your WORD, in Jesus name.

2. TO REVERSE NEGATIVE EFFECTS OF UNFULFILLED PLEDGES AND PROMISES

Heavenly Father, I come before You and confess my foolishness. Your Word says that those who don't fulfill their vows and pledges are fools and that You do not delight in them (Ecc. 5:4).

How foolish have I been all this while!

LORD, I am sorry for saying things and making commitments that I couldn't keep afterward. Please forgive and set me free from the limitations that this has brought on me, in Jesus name.

LORD, I ask You for grace and strength to obey Your Word henceforth. Help me by the Holy Spirit and keep me in constant reminder that I don't have to make promises and pledges to please men, but to please You.

As I begin to work towards fulfilling my pledges from today, grant me wisdom and speedy breakthrough, in Jesus name.

Deliverance by Fire

Every demon raising accusations against me in the spirit due to my past errors, comments, and unfulfilled pledges and promises, I attack you right now with God's Word.

Romans 8: 1- 2 says, "Therefore, there is now no condemnation for those who are in Christ because through Christ Jesus the law of the Spirit who gives life has set me free from the law of sin and death."

No demon has any ground to accuse me or bring an affliction against me. For I am now forgiven and set free by my Faith in Christ Jesus.

So I bind you unclean spirits of hate and lies against my life and destiny, and I cast you all into the abyss, in Jesus name.

With my mouth, I confess that I am seated with Christ in the heavenly places, far above all principalities and powers. I have been translated from the kingdom of darkness into the kingdom of Christ.

I am a bringer of light and a salter of lives and destinies. I am moving from glory to glory even now and forever, in Jesus name.

3. TO BREAK UNHOLY AGREEMENTS AND COVENANTS

Today, O Lord, I come against every negative agreement and covenant that I have entered into in the past, working against my life and destiny, by the Blood of Jesus Christ, I command these agreements and covenants to be broken, in Jesus name.

Every hidden evil covenant operating against my life and destiny, I renounce you, I reject you, and I command you to break now in Jesus name.

I nullify any evil covenant that I have been forced to enter through a dream or my ignorance.

I nullify any covenant between me and the powers of the Water, the air, the moon, the sun, the rock, and the land, in the mighty name of Jesus Christ.

Covenants made between me and any family idol and generational deities, be broken, in Jesus name.

By the Blood of Jesus Christ, I discontinue any covenant from my land of nativity affecting my glory and life.

Deliverance by Fire

Any evil covenant in the land or the foundation of the house where I am living right now, or I have ever lived before, affecting my life and destiny, be destroyed in Jesus name.

I plead the Blood of Jesus Christ over my spirit, soul, and body today.

I plead the Blood of Jesus Christ over my life and destiny.

I plead the Blood of Jesus Christ over my business and career.

I plead the Blood of Jesus Christ over my house and environment.

I plead the Blood of Jesus Christ over my tongue and entire body

By the Blood of Jesus Christ, I announce that I am no longer involved in any other covenant.

By the Blood of Jesus Christ, I am now in a new covenant of life, peace, divine health and prosperity with God the Father, God the Son and God the Holy Spirit, in Jesus name.

Thank You, Lord for answering my prayers, in Jesus name.

Amen.

FOR FURTHER READING

2 Samuel 18

Day 8: Killing Goliath: The Spirit of Fear

"While faith is the greatest force behind any victory in life, fear is the greatest force behind any defeat in life."

Goliath is a representation of the spirit of fear. Dealing with this spirit is important to walk in God's blessings.

As an authority in the occult, Goliath knew how to use the weapon of fear on his opponents. Once he had projected the spirit of fear on them through bold, oral intimidations, and curses, he made mincemeat of them in battle. Look at this instance:

> *Goliath stood and shouted to the ranks of Israel, "Why do you come out and line up for battle? Am I not a Philistine, and are you not the servants of Saul? Choose a man and have him come down to me*
> *- 1 Samuel 17:8*

Did you see that?

''Servants of Saul! ''

Is that who the Israelites were?

Of course not. But Goliath made them believe that. He made them forget they were servants of the MOST HIGH God. He talked them into forgetting that God who cannot be seen has helped them defeat bigger giants in their past. He made them look at themselves as ordinary servants of Saul.

And it worked. For as long as the Israelites saw themselves as too small to confront him, he was in charge.

> The spirit of fear will make you forget all the past victories and testimonies that God has given you. It will magnify situations before you and make it look like this is the end of the road.

The devil, working through fear, will do everything he can to make you think that you are a nobody; that you can't do anything; that you are just a small broom that will only get broken.

Goliath went on to intimidate the children of Israel. The Bible continues:

And the Philistine said, I defy the armies of Israel this day; give me a man, that we may fight together.
*When Saul and all Israel **HEARD THOSE WORDS** of the Philistine, they were dismayed and greatly afraid*

And all the men of Israel, when they saw the man, fled from him and were sore afraid. - **1 Samuel 17:10-11**

....

Goliath used fear to overrun the Israelites. With fear, he defeated them even before any strike. *"And all the men of Israel, when they saw the man, fled from him, and were sore afraid."*

I've learned that fear is a major threat to our life of victory in Christ. It is fear that makes people consult sorcerers for protection. It is fear that makes people not step out in faith to obey God's direction in their hearts. It is fear that makes people avoid making investments for their financial blessings.

Fear is something severe that God has over 365 fear not in the Bible for us. I want you to see fear as a great enemy and begin to address it like that from today.

A LESSON FROM THE FALL OF JERICHO

Rehab, the harlot from Jericho, confessed: ***I know that the Lord has given this land to you and that a great fear of you has fallen on us so that all who live in the country are melting in fear because of you*** - Joshua 2:8

That great city of Jericho had already been defeated even before the Israelites stepped on its shores. God had already sent fear and terror to the whole land of Jericho. They had lost the battle even before it was fought. That is God's plan in Exodus 23:27:

"I will send my terror ahead of you and throw into confusion every nation you encounter. I will make all your enemies turn their back and run."

God uses the weapon of fear on our enemies. Unfortunately, our enemies also try to use the weapon of fear on us. Any side that gets afraid loses the battle even before it is fought.

Notice how the people of Jericho contracted this fear that made them lose even before fighting. Rehab said:

We had **HEARD** how the Lord dried up the water of the Red Sea for you when you came out of Egypt, and what you did to Sihon and Og, the two kings of the Amorites east of the Jordan, whom you utterly destroyed
WHEN WE HEARD of it, our hearts melted in fear and everyone's courage failed because of you, for the Lord your God is God in heaven above and on the earth below - Joshua 2:9-11.

Note the bolded words. The people of Jericho got their fear from the NEWS they heard, and so lost, even without fighting. Of course, the fall of Jericho was part of God's plan for the lives of the Israelites, so that was a good outcome from our perspective. But there's some lesson to learn there as well.

The enemy is afflicting God's people with fear from WHAT THEY HEAR. Right from the news on TV, to news about witches, wizards, terrorists, occult men, etc. We become afraid and so lose our victory even before a fight takes place.

The truth is that the first cure for fear is to ***guard what you allow yourself to listen to***. I've found out that the news has a way of making us get annoyed and even afraid sometimes. Unfortunately, this innate fear weakens our victory gear in the face of life. We must learn to take the news with Faith, because as God's children, our words and thoughts are not to be decided by the news and stories that fly around, but by what God has said about us.

For example, never believe you are suffering from an incurable disease. That an expert with forty years of experience said so does not make it true. He has only done his best and doesn't know what to do next. Discover God's verdict before you conclude!

Experts may have the facts, but God has the final say.

FEAR OPENS DOOR FOR EVIL

The Bible says that when we serve God, He will bless our bread and water.

"And ye shall serve the Lord your God, and he shall bless thy bread, and thy water; and I will take sickness away from the midst of thee.

"There shall nothing cast their young, nor be barren, in thy land: the number of thy days I will fulfill.

"I will send my fear before thee and will destroy all the people to whom thou shalt come, and I will make all thine enemies turn their backs unto thee" - Exodus 23:25-27

Job was a servant of God. That was why he was so blessed to the extent he became the wealthiest man in the whole of the eastern part of the world during his time. But something happened, and he lost his wealth and was afflicted with a terrible illness.

Why did God allow such evil to visit Job suddenly? Why did sickness, death, and loss unexpectedly visit a man for whom it is written, "He feared God and shunned evil" (Job 1:1).

While the story of Job teaches us a great lesson in hope, it also has a lesson to teach us about fear. Job's fear was what opened the door for the devil to attack his life and family. He said:

What I feared has come upon me; what I dreaded has happened to me - **Job 3:25.**

Look at that. Yes, that's just a single verse. But it's there for us as well.

Job was serving God in fear, not the reverent fear of worship, but a fear that if he doesn't serve God that he would lose his wealth and suffer. He saw God as SOMEONE waiting for a person to make a mistake so He could punish him. All his sacrifices and acts of holiness were filled with... *"I just have to do this; else, if I make a mistake, sure, God might destroy my wealth."*

If he heard that his children went to a party, he would go and offer sacrifices, saying, who knows, they may have sinned. He was always afraid of disaster and failure. It was this constant fear that eventually opened the door for the devil to strike.

Job's story has more to teach us about the power of fear and partial belief, in addition to the other things we've taught from it. ***Job's fears were what opened the door for Satan.***

THE COMMAND TO FEAR NOT

"FEAR NOT" is one of the instructions required to enjoy God's blessings continually. For example, when God wanted to bless Hagar and Ishmael, her son, she was commanded to FEAR

NOT (Gen. 12:17). When God wanted to reaffirm His covenant with Abraham to Isaac, He commanded Isaac to FEAR NOT (Gen 26:24).

What about Joshua, David, Gideon, Jacob, Samuel, Hannah, Mary, Elisabeth, and the apostles? One of the instructions they were given to walk in God's covenant was FEAR NOT.

> **Fear disqualifies us from walking with God. It opens the door for evil spirits to attack us and cause other problems. It is the biggest weapon the enemy uses against us.**

Fear is so bad that the Bible puts the "FEARFUL" in the same category with adulterers, whoremongers, idolaters, and murderers (See Rev. 21:8). I perceive that God allowed Job to get some discipline so that, among other reasons, fear would be uprooted from his life.

WHAT YOU FEAR, YOU CREATE

The enemies of God's people always know that without making them afraid, they cannot capture them.

Deliverance by Fire

"Then they called out in Hebrew to the people of Jerusalem who were on the wall, to terrify them and make them afraid in order to capture the city." - **2 Chronicles 32:18**

Just look at that! They can only capture them if they have made them afraid.

What does that tell you?

Your enemy will first and foremost do things to make you afraid. It is when you now have some of those fears that he finally captures you in that very area you got afraid. If, for example, you allow the fear of death to dominate your thoughts, you'll create the death consequence before you know it. The fear of death does not stop death. It instead gives the death power to come quicker.

If you are always afraid that you may lose your job or wealth, sorry, you may lose it sooner, because that fear will make you unconsciously begin to do things that will make you lose it.

What I feared has come upon me; what I dreaded has happened to me - **Job 3:25.**

If an enemy wants to run you down and out, he merely does things to make you afraid. With that fear now operating in you, that enemy can now carry out his wish successfully.

So look deeply. What are you afraid of? It's time to deal with your fears.

It's true that what we fear and worry about are only in our heads. Most times they are not real. But the Bible also paints a clear picture that many times our fears and worries bring those consequences closer to our lives.

Our fears and worries give life to *consequences* that do not exist and empowers them to be created. While faith is the most significant force behind any victory in life, fear is the greatest force behind any defeat in life.

Your Goliaths are those voices shouting to you that you are doomed, that you will fail, that you won't succeed, that you will die in that illness, etc. Anything that is trying to show you how small you are is your Goliath.

Locate your Goliaths today and confront them. Those inner voices of fear and defeat, arise and shout at them to keep quiet. Tell them that you are going forward and that nothing will stop you. Let us deal with the spirit of fear today.

PRAYERS

1. *The Lord is my light and my salvation; whom shall I fear? The Lord is the strength of my life; of whom shall I be afraid?*

2. *When the wicked came against me to eat up my flesh, my enemies and foes, they stumbled and fell.*

Deliverance by Fire

~3~ *Though an army may encamp against me, my heart shall not fear; though war may rise against me, in this, I will be confident. - Psalm 27:1-3.*

I proclaim today that greater is He that is in me than any devil on the side of my enemies.

It is written that the righteous are as bold and daring as a lion.

By my trust in Christ Jesus, I am righteous. I, therefore, receive my divine boldness, in Jesus name.

The angels of the LORD encamp round about them that fear God. The archangels of God are with me; I have no reason to fear. I have no basis to worry or be depressed.

Every spirit of fear, worry, and panic in my life, I bind all of you and cast you all into the abyss, in the name of Jesus.

From today, I break every evil covenant that has brought fear, worry, and depression into my life.

I command every terror of the night and arrow of the day that has brought fear and worry into my life to stop and move from my environment, in the name of Jesus.

I command every human agent using the spirits of fear to terrify me in the night to stumble and fall, in the name of Jesus.

The fear, terror, and arrows of doubters and the world shall not be my portion.

My tomorrow is blessed in Christ Jesus; my future is secure and guaranteed. Therefore, you spirit that is in charge of the fear and worry of tomorrow in my life, I bind you, in the name of Jesus.

Because my destiny is attached to God, I decree that I can never fail.

I command every bondage I have subjected myself to out of fear, worry and depression, be broken in Jesus name.

Deliverance by Fire

All harmful doors that the spirit of fear, anxiety and depression has opened in my life and family, be closed right now, in the name of Jesus Christ.

Every disease, oppression, and hopelessness that came into my life as a result of fear and worry, disappear this moment, in the name of Jesus.

Every evil seed that has been planted into my life and family, as a result of fear, worry, and panic, I command them to be uprooted, in Jesus name.

From today, Lord, I refuse to be intimidated by any demonic nightmare. Let all the agents of darkness that appear in my dream to torment me disappear from now onwards in Jesus name.

I decree henceforth that I shall sleep and sleep in peace, and wake up with joy and peace all around me, in Jesus name.

Every enchantment and invocation of fear and worry being made against me, I neutralize you, and I command you to fail, in the name of Jesus.

Every alliance of the enemies in my home with the enemies outside shall not stand, in the name of Jesus.

I destroy all the labors of the enemy to frustrate my work.

I nullify every evil writing, agreement or covenant against my career, in the name of Jesus.

O LORD, it is written that You delight in my prosperity. Therefore, LORD, I pray that You bless me indeed in my career. Let no household foe be able to control my happiness any longer.

May all those who are against me without reason in my place of work turn back and be brought to confusion, in the name of Jesus.

My life is hidden with Christ in God. Therefore, no one can destroy me or harm me. No weapon of Satan and his agents formed against me shall prosper.

I command all doors leading to my blessings, victory, and breakthroughs which the enemies have closed before now, to be OPENED WIDE from today, in the name of Jesus.

Deliverance by Fire

Every territorial spirit employed against us in our neighborhood, be frustrated, bound and cast into the abyss, in the name of Jesus Christ.

Father, Lord, arrest, humiliate and neutralize every power contrary to Your name, operating in my house, environment, and neighborhood, in the Mighty name of Jesus Christ.

I bind the spirit of death, armed robbery, burglary, terror and assassination in my neighborhood, in the name of Jesus Christ.

I reject, forsake and destroy every evil agreement or covenant working against my family and this neighborhood.

By the blood of Jesus Christ, I nullify the effects and operation of evil forces around my house, in the name of Jesus.

O LORD, let all my stubborn pursuers of my life be occupied with unprofitable assignments.

Exposé and reveal the secrets of all my enemies masquerading as my friends, in Jesus name.

I am free from fear, worry, depression and panic attacks.

O Lord, let Your name be praised forever and ever in my life, in Jesus name.

Amen.

FOR FURTHER READING

1 Samuel 17

Day 9: Killing Jezebel: The Spirit of Witchcraft

Culled from my book, Prayers to Destroy Witchcraft

"And he made his children pass through the fire in the valley of the son of Hinnom: also he observed times, and used enchantments, and used witchcraft, and dealt with a familiar spirit, and with wizards: he wrought much evil in the sight of the LORD, to provoke him to anger." **- 2 Chron 33:6**

More people are suffering from witchcraft oppressions than we know and address today. For instance, each time I talk about witchcraft on our website, it generates a lot of feedbacks. In fact, over forty percent of the prayer requests we receive daily have to do with witchcraft of some sort. These stories of people have made me do a full book on witchcraft, and I'll be doing a whole month exposition on witchcraft on the website very soon.

Witchcraft is the use of power gained from evil spirits or demons to inflict harm, foretell events, control people or things, deceive, or conjure something. It can include the ability to control the powers of nature or someone else.

There's no difference between witchcraft, sorcery, divination, and magic. They all involve communicating with evil spirits and using their guidance to create good or bad situations, negative or positive experiences. The following words and their practices mean the same thing as witchcraft: magic (black magic, white magic), sorcery, divination, black arts, occultism, wizardry, witchery, witching, necromancy (communicating with the dead), voodooism, voodoo, hoodoo, palm reading, Wicca, natural magic, makutu; rarethaumaturgy, theurgy, the old religion, demonry, diablerie, sortilege, medium, astrology, new ageism, etc.

All of these and their accomplishments are witchcraft and attract the same divine judgment and consequences. They are not just some form of old religion or nature worship. The Bible forbids them and declares them as taboos.

9 "When you come into the land which the Lord your God is giving you, you shall not learn to follow the abominations of those nations. 10 There shall not be found among you anyone who makes his son or his daughter pass through the fire, or one who practices witchcraft, or a soothsayer, or one who interprets omens, or a sorcerer, 11 or one who conjures spells, or a medium, or a spiritist, or one who calls up the dead.

12 For all who do these things are an abomination to the Lord, and because of these abominations the Lord your God drives them out from before you. 13 You shall be blameless before the Lord your God. 14 For these nations which you will dispossess listened to soothsayers and diviners; but as for you, the Lord your God has not appointed such for you. –
(Deut.18:9-14)

Wikipedia, dictionaries, and witches may argue with you that witchcraft means something else. But God says that all forms of witchcraft are evil. I would rather listen to God than the world.

WHAT THE BIBLE SAYS ABOUT WITCHCRAFT

Witchcraft is from satan and anyone who practices it does what is abominable before God. If you know anyone involved in witchcraft or any of its associated practices (like sorcery, fortune telling, magic, palm reading, invocation of the dead, etc.), prayerfully attempt to help them save their lives, but if they refuse your help, stay away from them.

When we dabble in witchcraft, we open up ourselves to demons and their influences. We invite them to create spiritual and physical frustrations for us. We surrender to the leadership and control of the devil. We make ourselves lawful captives

Here are a few scriptures about witchcraft and all of its related practices. Anyone who reads these scriptures and still thinks that witchcraft is okay and normal should think again.

1. We are warned to stay away from any form of witchcraft

Leviticus 19:26 (NLT) - *Do not eat meat that has not been drained of its blood. Do not practice fortune-telling or witchcraft.*

Leviticus 19:31 (NIRV) - *Do not look for advice from people who get messages from those who have died. Do not go to people who talk to the spirits of the dead. If you do, they will make you unclean. I am the Lord your God.*

Leviticus 20:6 (NLT) - *I will also turn against those who commit spiritual prostitution by putting their trust in mediums or in those who consult the spirits of the dead. I will cut them off from the community.*

Leviticus 20:6 (NIRV) - *Suppose someone looks for advice from people who get messages from those who have died. Or they go to people who talk to the spirits of the dead. And they do what those people say. Then they have not been faithful to me. So I will turn against them. I will separate them from their people.*

Deuteronomy 18:10-13 - *There shall not be found among you anyone who makes his son or his daughter pass through the fire, or one who practices witchcraft, or a soothsayer, or* one who interprets omens, or a sorcerer, 11 or one who conjures spells, or a medium, or a spiritist, or one who calls up the dead. 12 For all who do these things are an abomination to the Lord, and because of these abominations the Lord your God drives them out from before you. 13 You shall be blameless before the Lord your God.

2. Practicing witchcraft leads to eternal damnation

Revelation 21:8 (NLT) - *But cowards, unbelievers, the corrupt, murderers, the immoral,* **those who practice witchcraft***, idol worshipers, and all liars-their fate is in the fiery lake of burning sulfur. This is the second death.*

Galatians 5:19-21 (ISV) - *Now the actions of the flesh are obvious: sexual immorality, impurity, promiscuity,* 20 *idolatry,* **witchcraft***, hatred, rivalry, jealousy, outbursts of anger, quarrels, conflicts, factions,* 21 *envy, murder, drunkenness, wild partying, and things like that. I am telling you now, as I have told you in the past, that people who practice such things will not inherit the kingdom of God.*

3. The consequence of practicing witchcraft is death.

Leviticus 20:26-27 (NLT) - *You must be holy because the Lord is holy. I have set you apart from all other people to be my very own. Men and women among you who act as* mediums or who consult the spirits of the dead must be put to death by stoning. They are guilty of a capital offense.

1 Chronicles 10:13-14 (NLT) - *So Saul died because he was unfaithful to the Lord. He failed to obey the Lord's command, and he even consulted a medium 14 instead of asking the Lord for guidance. So the Lord killed him and turned the kingdom over to David, son of Jesse.*

Exodus 22:18 – *Do not suffer a witch to live.*

Micah 3:7 (GWT) - *Seers will be put to shame. Those who practice witchcraft will be disgraced. All of them will cover their faces because God won't answer them.*

4. Trust God for guidance, not mediums

Isaiah 8:19-20 (NIRV) - *Some people get messages from those who have died. But these people only whisper words that are barely heard. Suppose someone tells you to ask for advice from these people. Shouldn't you ask for advice from your God instead? Why should you get advice from dead people to help those who are alive? [20] Follow what the Lord taught you and said to you through me. People who don't speak in keeping with these words will have no hope in the morning.*

Proverbs 3:5-8 *(TLB) - If you want favor with both God and man, and a reputation for good judgment and common sense, then trust the Lord completely; don't ever trust yourself. ₆ In everything you do, put God first, and he will direct you and crown your efforts with success.*

₇₋₈ Don't be conceited, sure of your own wisdom. Instead, trust and reverence the Lord, and turn your back on evil; when you do that, then you will be given renewed health and vitality.

....

As you can see, witchcraft is a serious issue. It is not what the world says it is. It is not what movies and films say it is. The first step to dealing with witchcraft is to understand what it is in all its ramifications according to Scriptures. By being able to comprehend witchcraft, we can first and foremost separate ourselves from its appearances and manifestations. Then we can pray and renounce its activities against us.

TYPES OF WITCHCRAFT

Witchcraft practitioners don't believe they are evil. They think that we do not understand witchcraft and its goodness. They believe that witchcraft itself is used to create benefits, inventions, and progress in the society. They feel that those who hurt others in their rituals and worships are a different set of witches and don't practice real witchcraft. They want us to accept witchcraft as a way to make progress

However, the Bible calls all forms of witchcraft evil. Anything that involves controlling of others, casting spells, all types of rituals, the Bible calls them evil and abomination.

Here are my different forms of witchcraft:

1. Ignorant (Blind) Witchery

It is possible that one indulges in witchcraft without knowing what he or she is doing. Those who practice modern day magic, and use it as fun, are practicing witchcraft unknowingly. Those who are buying books, courses and tutorials, learning and trying different witchcraft essentials, like invocations, casting spells, magic, air dance, fire dance, disappearing, conjuring things, etc. are involving themselves in witchcraft unknowingly.

Those who are joining secret societies, Eastern Star, Freemasons, Lodge, and so on, are also involving in witchcraft. Yes, it's possible that one sees these organizations as just a group for socialization, learning, and personal improvement. However, their basic tenets of faith deny the deity of Jesus Christ and the Trinity. So whatever they are doing as benefits are just a cover-up for what they are in reality. Membership in them is, before God, a form of witchcraft.

Consulting fortune tellers, sorcerers, necromancers, spiritists, palm readers, and magicians for some kind of solution to life problems is also another way to involve in witchcraft unknowingly. Note that just because you have a problem and needed help, and so consults these mediums does not exonerate you from witchcraft. The Bible warns us against seeking means other than God through Jesus Christ for spiritual help and solution.

Another way people let the spirit of witchcraft use them unknowingly is by:

- Bullying others
- Gossip
- Talking down on others
- Murder
- Intimidation
- Lack of empathy

People who display these tendencies are unknowingly exhibiting witchcraft. The spirit of witchcraft is using them because witchcraft is about suppression, wickedness, and intimidation.

Whether one knows it or not while practicing witchcraft, the Bible clearly warns against witchcraft, in fact, often pronouncing harsh judgments for those who practice it.

2. Intentional Witchcraft

These are hardcore witches who use the practice of witchcraft to hurt others. They were either initiated into witchcraft by their earlier generations or through some contact with other witches. Either way, they are carrying out their acts intentionally. Their goal is to steal, to kill and to destroy. They may have been promised considerable rewards in their witchcraft covens and worship centers if they do more harm to their family members and to others.

These types of witches act upon the instruction and lies of the devil to perpetrate a lot of wickedness in the society, albeit secretly. We can destroy the limitations raised against us by this kind of witchcraft only with serious warfare prayers.

Read this story below:

Deliverance by Fire

....

"Hello all, my name is........................

"12 years ago my mother-in-law came to visit her three children who lived in London. She came from West Africa. I am married to his oldest son, and she will take turns in staying with her kids. From the very first night she stayed in my house, things changed for me forever.

We were born-again Christians, and we were very prayerful as a family. We had two boys, and a girl and the children were very young when she came.

My husband who was a role model for other young men suddenly began to sleep around. It was so bad that he started drinking and out of frustration, I joined in too.

"My husband will pray with me and then open a bottle of wine and make sure I drank enough to put me to sleep so he can spend the night in other woman's bed, sometimes only a few streets away.

"So much happened, I saw the face of the devil in this man. I returned to prayers and worship. One day his mom came over while I was watching GOD Chanel. 30 minutes into the programme a prayer was said for viewers. By the time I said amen, my mother-in-law had started confessing to witchcraft.

"She told me her father who had long passed away was a cripple to the mortal eye but a king in the witchcraft Kingdom. She said that she is a princess in her father's Kingdom. She described in detail how she and her dad operated and even said her dad had a cat which was used for all sort of things. When her dad needed to use the toilet, he passed it by witchcraft to the cat who then went for him.

"Some of the secret she revealed where so frightening. I should have left his son instantly because what 69 year old will lie about something like that? But I had no money.

Our business went under, we lost all our investments, both our cars broke down without explanation and could not be repaired but once we sold it for parts one buy went in the car, and it just worked so he drove away.

This is a car that was seen by three different mechanics. Oh my God, did my life go to hell!!!! The son promoted from sleeping out to bringing his lovers in my house. The things that have happened to me in the last five years were even worst. I can write a whole book or two!!!

I started having horrible dreams; I began behaving erratically going on the internet to find help and buying books etc. In short, I lost my home, my job and on the 19th of March 2012 I found my 14 year old dead on the floor in his room. Since then I stopped living. I look so old due to self-neglect. If it was not for my other two who are both in university I would have killed myself.

"The sadness in my heart is overwhelming. I can't listen to music, praise and worship time in church is so painful. I cry to GOD every day. Why has God abandoned me like this? I pray but get no answer! I pray for my children all the time yet God allow this much suffering for my life.

If there is anyone out there who God listens to PLEASE HELP ME!
God bless you all.

....
I hear stories like this almost every day. Many times, I want to disbelieve them. But the truth is that you can't take people's experiences away from them.

It is possible that people involved in witchcraft are carrying out evil practices against others unknowingly. They may have been promised huge rewards to attack their loved ones and deceived in their witchcraft meetings, that by hurting their loved ones, they are helping them. Sadly, they are only a part of Satan's mission to steal, kill and destroy.

And let me say this:

> *If things are always breaking down in your life and home without any justifiable reason, that is a witchcraft attack. Stop quarreling and fighting. Learn to return fire until they seize.*

3. People Possessed With the Spirit of Witchcraft

These are people we may say have attitude problems. The Bible references this class of witchcraft under the works of the flesh in Galatians 5: 19 -20:

> [19]*Now the actions of the flesh are manifest, which are these: Adultery, fornication, uncleanness, lasciviousness,* [20]*Idolatry, witchcraft, hatred, variance, emulations, wrath, strife, seditions, heresies.*

A more in-depth look will reveal that these people are possessed by the spirit of witchcraft. As stated above, these people like to domineer and control others. They believe their words are the ultimate and seldom take corrections. They are bullies and celebrate when they cause others pains.

If you're in a relationship or working with someone who treats you like a piece of trash, suppresses your views and demands your worship (directly or indirectly) as a way to get along, then this person is under the influence of witchcraft spirit. He or she may not be the real problem. You have to take authority against the spirit of witchcraft and break the control.

4. Charismatic Witchcraft

Charismatic witchcraft is exercising control over other Christians by leaders or anyone within the church, using personal prophecy or visions or other methods. Its intent revolves around domination, intimidation, manipulation, monetary profit, and emotional blackmail.

Many innocent Christians are suffering from one kind of affliction or the other because they submitted themselves to spiritual wolves in one way or the other. Not until recently when the LORD began to open my eyes did I start learning the danger posed by these lazy, pretentious, demonic men, who often pose as men and women of God. Beyond the risk of leading people away from the LORD, these wolves can also be a gateway for the imposition of spiritual obstacles against God's people.

Read this letter:

"Thank you for opening our eyes.
"A lady did deliverance on me. She laid her hands on my eyes and prayed for healing; there was nothing wrong with my eyes. My eyes

started scratching terribly and have continued to do so for 3 and half years. My eyes have even become droopy, and sometimes I can't sleep because of the scratching in my eyes. I have asked forgiveness and prayed every deliverance prayer, but somehow nothing has helped. I believe this woman used charismatic witchcraft. My personality has never been the same after that. I can literally feel demons move around my eyes. How do I get them out?? I was a month old Christian when this happened. Does anyone know how to fix my eyes?" - Louwna

These men and women come with enticing words and visions and prophecies, and it's mostly difficult to decipher their real intent on a first look. They give visions and prophecies and lure ignorant Christians to their bidding. That is why we are warned not be carried away by prophecies and visions, especially prophecies and visions that don't have any Biblical basis.

For example, a young man visited our family friend some time ago, in the guise of the Lord asking him to come and pray for them and break the curse of barrenness on the woman. He was warmly welcomed and given room to stay as much as he wanted and carry out his prayers and spiritual operations. Unfortunately, before long, he had started sleeping with the young maids in the house and building various degrees of soul ties with them.

Another so-called "prophet of God" told a beloved sister that her husband is in the occult, that she would need to steal the man's SUV and bring it to him and divorce the man. Sadly, the sister took her husband's SUV and left the house with a note...in the bidding of the so-called "prophet."

The other day too, my friend's wife was told that her husband was not God's will for her. That she needed to marry someone else to be able to fulfill God's plans for her life.

Imagine that!

No doubt, we are in a prophetic age. This is the age of the spirit of visions and prophecy. But we have to watch it carefully because Satan too has trickily gotten involved.

Most times the ultimate goal of these demonic men is their belly - to make a profit. So even in the visions and prophecies they give, there are no real solutions in them, but just monetization opportunities.

Am I against spiritual gifts, visions, prophecies and seeing in the spirit?

Absolutely no.

But we have to discern all spirits as the Bible says. Not just because of the dangers so visible as I've shared, but because these prophecies and visions and what follows them have the potential of eventually becoming a source of satanic oppressions against a person.

Maybe you've submitted yourself to spiritual wolves in the past who gave you false prophecies, and you acted on them, laid hands on you and even led you to do some unsuspecting rituals. It's time to go before God and plead for restoration.

5. Self-Witchcraft

Rebellion is willful disobedience to God's revealed voice, instruction, leading and direction for one's life. The Bible considers this as equivalent to witchcraft. That's because the person tries to witchcraft (control) God to work in some way different from how God is leading. This was the primary reason for Saul's rejection as the king of Israel. 1 Samuel 15:23 says:

> *"For rebellion is as the sin of witchcraft, and stubbornness is as iniquity and idolatry. Because thou hast rejected the word of the LORD, he hath also rejected thee from being king."*

Rebellion was also what led to Jonah being swallowed by a fish. He would have been destroyed if not that he repented in the fish's belly.

One thing about the sin of willfully disobeying God's revealed voice to you is that no one will have the solution to your problem or situation. You'll pray and pray, make confessions, sow seeds, but will not get help and answers; because you are trying to get God to move in other ways different from His direction which has been revealed to you, and which you know. It's only in repentance and humble submission that you'll get help and answers to your situation.

HOW TO KNOW IF YOU'RE UNDER A WITCHCRAFT ATTACK

To understand how the spirit of witchcraft works, let's look at the activities of Biblical Jezebel, which is used as a representation of the spirit of witchcraft

Jezebel was the chief priestess of the cult of Baal worship, which dominated the city of Tyre. She influenced her husband, Ahab, into taking very deadly decisions that not only hurt others but also destroyed them. She introduced Baal worship in Israel and created spiritual limitations that locked the Israelites out of their blessings all through her reign. Some of the tendencies this witch woman manifested include:

- Seduction

- Control

- Domineering

- Lack of empathy.

- Willfully hurting others

- Working for and celebrating the downfall of someone

- Disregard for God

- Causing disfavor for others.

- Murder

- Taking what belongs to others forcefully

- Etc.

Those are precisely what the witchcraft spirit tries to achieve against people. For example, if you are being seduced by someone (male or female) in a very uncontrollable, unexplainable, pulling, overpowering way, the person may be possessed with the spirit of Jezebel and trying to pull you down.

If you are dealing with someone who displays strong tendencies of being domineering, unchallengeable, *my-word-is-the-ultimate* kind, the person is undoubtedly living with a Jezebel (witchcraft) spirit.

A person possessed with the spirit of Jezebel displays domineering and controlling tendencies. They rarely show remorse for their mistakes. They are secretly or even openly happy when others are hurt. They have a brazen disregard and often mock the things of God and are delighted to celebrate the downfall of God's people.

> The spirit of Jezebel (witchcraft) works and derives pleasure when people are hurt. It shows no empathy for anyone who is not doing as it wants.

The spirit of witchcraft will magnify a little mistake or even an outright lie and use it to create so much emotional hurt for its target, all with the intention to pull the person down.

The ultimate goal of witchcraft is to harm a person, either directly or indirectly.

If you are experiencing extreme disfavor from people; whatever you do, no matter how sincere you are and how much exceptional effort you put in, it doesn't make sense; the spirit of witchcraft may have been unleashed against you.

Here are other signs that you may be under a witchcraft attack:

- Unusual influence over you to please someone even when the premise is wrong

- Extraordinary intimidation and threat causing you to fear and to follow along and comply without questioning

- Feeling of or being controlled to do things you would not have done in your real and rational self.

- Extreme disfavor and non-appreciation of your positive contributions

- The sudden collapse of your sources of income or health without a reasonable explanation..

- Constant attacks and beatings in dreams.

- Seeing cats, dogs and other strange animals in dreams.

- Waking up sickly, especially after eating in the dream or being attacked.

- Choking sensations or feeling of being strangled and subdued while sleeping and struggling to move or get up.

- Things are always breaking and spoiling in your home.

There may be other ways that witchcraft spirit may be working against someone that we may not have listed here. If you have a suspicion that you may be under a witchcraft attack, then brace up.

PRAYERS

1. Against Charismatic Witchcraft

Most Gracious Father, once again I come to You today and declare my total surrender to THEE.

I declare that no one else is the LORD and savior of my life, except Jesus Christ, Your Most begotten Son.

LORD, I ask You to forgive me, in any way I have surrendered myself to men and women who come in YOUR name but are using evil powers. I believe I didn't listen enough to You, which was why I submitted to their tricks.

I believe You tried to warn me, but perhaps I placed my own needs far above Your instruction.

Heavenly Father, just like the prodigal son, I come back and ask for forgiveness. For the sake of the shed Blood of Jesus Christ, please forgive me, in Jesus name.

Father LORD, I'm now asking for total restoration.

You said in Joel 2:25-26, **"And I will restore to you the years that the locust hath eaten, the cankerworm, and the caterpillar, and the palmerworm, my great army which I sent among you.**

"And ye shall eat in plenty, and be satisfied, and praise the name of the LORD your God, that hath dealt wondrously with you: and my people shall never be ashamed."

LORD, please restore to me my health, peace of mind, fruitfulness, prosperity, and breakthrough. Restore to me whatever has been tampered with in my life as a result of the witchcraft of false preachers and visioners, in Jesus name.

Father, I stand in authority in the name of Jesus Christ and bind every demon released into my life, family, home, marriage, and business, by wolves in sheep's clothing. I

Deliverance by Fire

command these demons to pack their loads and leave my life right now and go back into the abyss, in Jesus name.

I break every tie and spiritual connection between me and demons projected through demonic men and women of God, in Jesus name.

I command every evil deposit in my life and family by false preachers and teachers to be destroyed by fire this day, in Jesus name.

O LORD, Correct every wrong mindset I have accepted from false, pretentious preachers and teachers that are working against my life and destiny, in Jesus name.

I declare a total restoration and healing of any part of my life that have been tampered with by my ignorant submission to these appealing deceivers, in Jesus name.

Dear Holy Spirit, Jesus said that You would teach me all things and bring everything to my remembrance.

I am truly sorry in any way I have grieved You in the past by not paying attention to what You were asking me to do and avoid.

Please Holy Spirit, kindly forgive me in Jesus name.

I am now asking You to restore and revive my spiritual antenna. Give me instant alerts whenever I am standing before a wolf in sheep's clothing, and give me the strength to follow Your leading henceforth, in Jesus name.

2. Judgment on Witchcraft

Heavenly Father, I thank You for giving me authority and power to defeat the kingdom of darkness. I thank You for the authority that I have in Christ Jesus to overcome and defeat witchcraft, Jezebel and the devil their father.

Through Our LORD and Savior Jesus Christ, You have given me the authority to trample on snakes and scorpions and to overcome all the power of the enemy, and nothing will harm me (Luke 10:19).

Lord, You have decreed that whatever I bind on earth will be bound in heaven, and whatever I loose on the earth will be loosed in heaven, and that if two of us on the earth agree *about anything we ask for, it will be done for us exactly as we agreed* (Matthew 18:18-19).

Today, Heavenly Father, I am in agreement with Jesus. I agree with the Holy Spirit. And I agree with Your WORD.

I have authority and power over the spirits of witchcraft, Jezebel, wickedness and disfavor. I have dominion over the decisions and activities of the powers of darkness at all levels

As I stand in this perfect agreement and pray and confess this day, I accept my victory over witchcraft and their works in my life and family in Jesus name.

O LORD, there can be no two kings over my life and family. There can be no two masters and influencers over my destiny and my family.

Jesus Christ is the ONLY LORD of my life, my destiny, and my family. He is the Only One with the right to access and direct my thoughts, my family, and my destiny.

So I reject every form of exercise of authority of the devil and the witchcraft world over my life and family this day and forever, in Jesus name.

I plead the Blood of Jesus Christ right now over my spirit, soul, and body.

I plead the Blood of Jesus Christ over my home, my family and my neighborhood.

I plead the Blood of Jesus Christ over everything that concerns me today and forever.

By the Blood of Jesus Christ, I declare my victory over witchcraft, the spirit of Jezebel and the devil himself, in Jesus name.

Heavenly Father, according to Your WORD, Let the walls and defenses of witchcraft against my life, my destiny, and my family be torn down and let every form of witchcraft against me be put to an end from this day and forever, in Jesus name.

O LORD, frustrate every witch, every wizard, every Jezebel, and every fortune teller against my life and family, in Jesus name.

Deliverance by Fire

Let disgrace and shame become the lot of witches and wizards working against my life at any level from today and forever, in Jesus name.

Father in the name of Jesus Christ, I speak into the spirit world this day; I speak into the air; I speak into the land, and I speak into the sea. I speak into the four corners of the earth, and I speak into all spiritual kingdoms that are not seen by man.

I command fire from heaven to scatter every evil gathering of witches and wizards and wicked men and women against my life and family, every kind of meeting that has taken place or will take place ever again. I command them to scatter and be destroyed by fire from heaven, in Jesus name.

I break the power of witchcraft's deception, seduction, sorcery, domination, and intimidation over my life and family, in the name of Jesus Christ.

Every seat of witchcraft in my household, be destroyed by fire right now, in Jesus name.

O LORD, let every evil instrument of witchcraft deposited in my life and family catch fire right now and be destroyed.

It is written, "Every plant that God has not planted shall be rooted out" (Matthew 15:13).

I, therefore, command every evil seed in the form of strife, quarrels, disfavor, hatred, nightmares, illnesses, disappointments, and confusions planted in my life, against my life or in my family to be uprooted by fire this moment, in Jesus name.

May whatever I have eaten out of ignorance that was a connecting point between me and witchcraft manipulation be exposed and purged out of my life and family, and destroyed by Fire, in Jesus name.

O LORD, let every witchcraft instrument, arrows, covens, pots, rings, books, clothes, being used against my family and me, or in my possession, knowingly or unknowingly, let them catch fire this moment and burn to ashes in Jesus name.

I reverse all witchcraft curses, covenants, spells and incantations against my life and family this day.

Deliverance by Fire

I command God's blessings of love, favor, prosperity and abundant life to replace every evil pronouncement and decree made against my family and me by witches, wizards and people with the spirit of Jezebel, in Jesus name.

O LORD, Because the hearts of men and kings are in Your Hands and You turn them wherever pleases YOU (Proverbs 21:1); I ask that from today, YOU turn the hearts of men and women to work for my favor and progress wherever I go, in Jesus name.

Whatever I have lost, and whatever have been denied me in life as a result of the activities of witchcraft and wicked forces of darkness or evil men, I claim a seven-fold restoration this day, in Jesus name.

O LORD, I lift up my spouse, family, and children before You. I lift up our career, our ministry, our business, our community and our neighbors before You. I break the bonds of darkness, witchcraft, and Jezebel over them, and I set them free to serve God, in Jesus name.

LORD, I thank You for delivering me from the power of witchcraft and blessing me with favor and peace round about. I thank You for restoring my home and surrounding my family with Your kindness and presence. May You alone be glorified and praised forever and ever, in Jesus name.

FOR FURTHER READING

1 Kings 16:31; 18:4-19; 19:1, 2; 21:5-25; 2 Kings 9

Day 10: Killing Pharaoh: Stubborn Destiny Chasers

₂"*Son of man, set your face against Pharaoh king of Egypt, and prophesy against him, and against all Egypt.* ₃*Speak, and say, 'Thus says the Lord God:*

"Behold, I am against you, O Pharaoh king of Egypt, O great monster who lies in the midst of his rivers, Who has said, 'My river is my own; I have made it for myself.'

₄*But I will put hooks in your jaws, and cause the fish of your rivers to stick to your scales; I will bring you up out of the midst of your rivers, and all the fish in your rivers will stick to your scales.*

₅*I will leave you in the wilderness, you and all the fish of your rivers; you shall fall on the open field; You shall not be picked up or gathered. I have given you as food to the beasts of the field and the birds of the heavens.* - **Ezekiel 29:2-5**

Pharaoh is a representation of the spirit of bondage, slavery, oppression, stubbornness, denial, recurring affliction, and hard-heartedness. You remember that Pharaoh refused to let the Israelites go even after mighty miraculous demonstrations. And even when he permitted for them to go, he eventually changed his mind and pursued them.

If you're confronted with situations and problems that refuse to go, even after many prayers, *fastings*, prophetic declarations, and many people praying for you, then you may be facing a situation orchestrated by the spirit of Pharaoh. Here are a few signs of situations perpetrated by a Pharaoh spirit.

Affliction from childhood

Pharaoh was the one who gave an order that all male children of the Israelites should be killed; baby Moses would have been eliminated if not for God's intervention.

The spirit of Pharaoh is the spirit of destiny termination. The spirit of Pharaoh aims at killing the next generation. They want to stop people from fulfilling their destinies.

Afflictions, pains and specific sufferings that start from childhood and continue into one's adulthood are carried out by the spirit of Pharaoh. Such afflictions are intended to thwart a person's destiny, to prevent the person from amounting to anything in life. These childhood-to-adulthood afflictions usually defy many prayers, and efforts for a solution, until God's revelation, power, and judgments are invoked.

Hardness of heart

There are not many people who will witness the kind of miracles and power demonstrations that Pharaoh saw, through Moses, and remained unmoved. It took the death of his son to get him to allow his captives to go. And he would later change his mind and still pursued them.

If you're dealing with someone who seems to have an unusual hardness of heart, that person may be under the influence of the spirit of pharaoh. Many hardened criminals are under the control of the spirit of pharaoh. Pharaoh's heart was so hardened that the Lord had to bombard him with ten dangerous plagues, and even after the ten plagues, he remained hardened until the red sea encounter.

Some problems and situations in your life need a red sea encounter.

Some problems are orchestrated by strongmen in the spirit of Pharaoh. They want to keep their captives forever. They resist all kinds of prayers unless serious judgments from heaven judge them. It can get so severe and recurrent that the persons involved will eventually accept their problem as a part of life. Sometimes these persistent spiritual strongmen persist in carrying out their afflictions because they had a legal right in the person's life or family. Most generational problems that persist and never let go are because they had a legal right into the family or the individual's life. Until the things that gave these demons legal ground into the family is discovered and removed, they'll persist. The demons behind the afflictions are in the category of the spirit of pharaoh – very stubborn and persistent demons.

Recurrent affliction

Another thing that the spirit of pharaoh can cause is recurrent affliction. That is, an affliction that keeps coming back again and again. You may pray for a situation, and it goes, then after some time, it comes back again and becomes worse than before. That is a sign of the pharaoh spirits at work.

When Moses confronted pharaoh at first for the release of the Israelites, instead of reasoning with Moses, he increased their suffering.

₄Then the king of Egypt said to them, "Moses and Aaron, why do you take the people from their work? Get back to your labor." ₅And Pharaoh said, "Look, the people of the land are many now, and you make them rest from their labor!"
₆So the same day Pharaoh commanded the taskmasters of the people and their officers, saying, ₇"You shall no longer give the people straw to make brick as before. Let them go and gather straw for themselves. ₈And you shall lay on them the quota of bricks which they made before. You shall not reduce it. For they are idle; therefore they cry out, saying, 'Let us go and sacrifice to our God.' ₉ Let more work be laid on the men, that they may labor in it, and let them not regard false words." **– Exodus 5:4-9**

The demons of pharaoh increase one's sufferings when they sense that their captives are pleading for freedom in the spirit. I have seen people who start to pray for deliverance only for the situations they are praying to be free from increase in many ways. Someone once said to me, *"why is it that each time someone prays for me, my situation gets worse?"* You will agree with me that it's not God who increases her suffering. The thing is that these demons know when a person is tired of their situation and wants to be free. They will go all out to make you feel that the prayers you are making are the reason the problems are increasing. They are the spirits of pharaoh.

The spirit of mockery and arrogance

The spirit of pharaoh is also the spirit of mockery. They represent enemies who believe they can do anything and nothing will happen. When told about God, they would mock and jest about it.

When Moses went to Pharaoh and pleaded to let the Israelites go, he said, "Who is the Lord that I should obey His voice to let Israel go? I do not know the Lord, nor will I let Israel go." That's another way of saying, *"I don't believe your God can do anything. I'll not stop attacking and oppressing you. Just get out."*

It was only at the red sea that Pharaoh finally let the Israelites go. I repeat, **every stubborn enemy of your life needs a red sea encounter**. They won't let you go by praying, *"Lord, I'm suffering so much. I need help."* No. You have to demand justice and begin to release fire from heaven to swallow every projection of the spirit of pharaoh against your life and family. God has sent us Christ, and in his death and resurrection lies all the help we'll ever need.

Pharaohs are gods

In ancient Egypt, Pharaohs are seen as gods. They are worshipped. They do not operate a democratic government. They are dictators.

The spirit of pharaoh possesses all modern day dictators. If you're in a relationship where the partner behaves like a dictator, you need to take authority against the spirit of pharaoh. If you work with a boss who is a dictator, take authority against the spirit of pharaoh in that company.

The goal of every pharaoh is to be worshipped and served without questions. So anyone who acts in such a way is under the influence of the spirit of pharaoh. Don't go fighting the person physically, begin to take authority against the demons.

Employment of sorcerers

A pharaoh can go to any length to keep his captive. They employ the services of the best sorcerers, witches, and spiritists to keep their targets in perpetual suffering. When Moses approached Pharaoh for the freedom of the Israelites and did some miracles, pharaoh tried to match it with wonders from his paid sorcerers as well. He had the best dreamers, sorcerers, witches, and magicians in his payroll.

Certain individuals can be possessed with the spirit of pharaoh that they will go to any length to seek spiritual powers to harm their targets, keep them perpetually in slavery and oppression. They are always going from one spiritualist to the other seeking powers to deal with their targets. These people need persistent prayers of judgment to destroy their activities and obtain freedom in Christ.

Emotional Harassment

Pharaoh would see a plague, and say, *"Moses, come, please stop this plague and take your people away."* When Moses stops the plague, he would say, *"You guys ain't going nowhere."* He kept them under constant emotional torture. One minute he would say, "Okay, go." Another minute he would say, "No way! Go back to your work. I ain't letting you go."

Watch it. Whatever is responsible for your constant emotional harassment may be the work of the spirit of pharaoh. It's time to take authority and start releasing fire. Your pharaohs must die.

Oppression - hard labor

Pharaoh is the lord of taskmasters who cause people much pain and sorrow. Pharaoh represents the spirit of slavery, abuse, and grief. The spirit of pharaoh is controlling whatever situation in your life that poses a great threat and has refused to leave even after too many prayers. Buckle up and start demanding freedom by fire and by force.

Pursuers unto death

A lady called me one day and said, *"Sir, there is a big bird following me up and down. I was in Warri, I always saw this bird. Then I went to Port Harcourt, and I will always see this same bird following me."*

As at the time we were talking she had packed out of her husband's house because her husband was now living with their landlady in the same compound where they lived. I can't imagine how a full grown man will leave his wife and children, climb upstairs and start to live with his landlady lover, in the same building. That's not ordinary. The witch landlady was using witchcraft to pursue this lady and monitor her for destruction.

A lot of people are being pursued without knowing it, and by what they don't know, and as a result, many things happen in their lives that they can't explain. Their spiritual lives never catch fire because their pursuers create all manner of distractions, pleasures and false hopes that keeps them perpetually in their control. Their marriages are always having a crisis; their health is always suffering; their finances are always in tethers.

There are stubborn spiritual pursuers. Their goal is to the death, nothing else. The spirit of pharaoh possesses these pursuers. It's time to say, *"O Lord, arise and swallow all pursuers and chasers of my life and destiny, in Jesus name."*

How to Pray Through the Spirit of Pharaoh

Are you suffering from the operation of the spirit of pharaoh at the moment? Are there situations in your life that have defied many prayers and efforts? Do you sense that your destiny, ministry, family, career, and life are under constant attack, always moving from one crisis to the other?

One thing is sure. God can bring you deliverance. Yes, situations and circumstances caused by the spirit of pharaoh can be very stubborn, but they can be dealt with.

STEP ONE:

The first step to effectively deal with the spirit of pharaoh is to discover legal grounds that these demons could be using against you. As we noted on Day two, certain things can be an opening for spiritual pharaohs to have power over your life.

Review your past life with the help of the Holy Spirit. Have you intentionally or unintentionally entered into any evil covenant in the past? Did you have a sexual relationship with people who were possessed? Do you have a history of childhood illness or affliction that made your parents take you to all manner of places for help? Did your parents curse you? Did you at any time in your life visit a diviner, charmer, white garment church, river worshippers, etc.? Ask yourself critical questions and accept responsibility.

If you discover specific sins, confess them and repent. If you discover relationships and soul ties, break free from them and re-commit your life to Christ. If you find out materials and objects used in satanic worship, ask for wisdom and deal with them. If you uncover attitude issues like, receive grace to make amends.

STEP TWO:

Seek revelation. I do not mean that you should go from place to place looking for prophecies. No. Go to God and ask for supernatural insight as to why the situations have refused to move. If you have repented many times and attempted to remove things you feel are responsible for a situation, yet it doesn't go, then you have to change your prayers from commanding the situation to asking the Lord for revelation on what to do, how to pray, and any direction to follow. Turn **Jeremiah 33:3** into a prayer bullet and continue to wait on the Lord until He reveals to you great and mighty things that you do not know about the situation.

No pharaoh can withstand prayers inspired by divine revelations. Moses was able to bring judgment on Pharaoh through revelation-inspired actions of faith.

STEP THREE:

Finally, attack the spirit of pharaoh with God's prophetic word and bring the situations created by the demons into the courtroom of heaven.

Ezekiel chapter 29:2-5 gives an explicit instruction of prophetic declarations you must make against Pharaoh and Egypt. You must wake up in the midnight and begin to make these declarations and persist until justice is done.

PRAYERS

Pray these prayers in the midnight

....

Heavenly Father, I pray for Your revelation and insight into the situations in my life right now. According to Jeremiah 33:3, I pray Lord, show me things I do not know about the stubborn attacks in my life and family.

How do I overcome these situations, Lord?

Deliverance by Fire

(Mention what circumstances in your life are stubbornly refusing to leave)

What do I do? Teach me by Your Holy Spirit and inspire me with actions that will lead to my total freedom in Jesus name.

Precious Father, I take responsibility for anything I have done in the past that may be a legal ground for the powers of Pharaoh to war against my life and family. I come to You by the cleansing power of the Blood of Jesus Christ and receive total forgiveness and cleansing, in the name of Jesus Christ.

Today, Lord, I declare, no spirit of Pharaoh has any more right to dictate the events of my life. May whatever evil connecting between me and Egypt be destroyed today, in Jesus name.

Today, O Lord, I set my face against all demonic pharaohs and the company of Egypt against my life and family. I prophesy against the powers of Pharaoh and speak God's judgment on them from this day forward. May their strengths fail them. May their fishes die, and may their rivers turn to blood. May they become confused and be consumed by their own activities in Jesus name.

O Lord, my God, Let fire from heaven rain upon every witch, occult man, sorcerer or magician employed against my life and family. May fire also rain upon any man or woman who is engaging the services of witches and agents of darkness against me, in the name of Jesus Christ.

Today, Lord, I speak directly to all the demons that represent pharaohs in my life, finances, career, ministry, and family. Because God does not sanction their wicked activities, they will no longer continue in my life and destiny. I command them to become crippled today, bound and cast into the abyss, in Jesus name.

May every stubborn pursuer and chaser of my life and destiny be swallowed by the river of judgment. May every spirit of a pharaoh from my family background perish in the red sea of judgment in Jesus name.

Deliverance by Fire

Father, I present the following situations before You once again.

(Mention specific stubborn problems that have refused to go away from your life.)

O Lord, I bring these issues before Your courtroom. I remind these situations that the Blood of Jesus Christ has secured my freedom on the cross. So they have no right to refuse to leave. I, therefore, speak to these problems to end today, in Jesus name.

For as long as no one can argue the death and resurrection of Christ, no demon, man or woman, can argue my deliverance and freedom in Christ. I will not accept any situation that is not God's full and abundant life for me.

Thank You, Lord for Your power at work in my life to overcome and live a victorious life, in Jesus name.

FOR FURTHER READING

Exodus 5, 6, 7, 14, 15

Day 11: Overcoming the Forces of Delay and Denial

Culled from my post on the blog, www.betterlifeworld.org

Hope deferred makes the heart sick: but when the desire cometh, it is a tree of life. – Proverbs 13:12

When prayers are delayed or denied, who is responsible?

Is it God?

Or the devil?

Or us?

The answer is simple. All of the above can be responsible.

UNDERSTANDING WHEN DELAYS ARE FROM GOD

Sometimes, delays can be from God. Other times they are caused by us, and many times they can be from the devil. God's delays are usually a time of going through a process of growth and development.

For instance, if you started a business last month, there's no way that the business will become global in three months. The company needs time to grow and develop. It has to go through a process. While you slog towards the bigger pictures in your mind, the business continues to make daily, weekly and yearly progress.

That normal process of gradual growth and development is what I call divine delays – God taking you through a process - or better put, productive patience. That is, while you're patient, you're also making progress.

But when you're stuck and stagnated, that's demonic. When you go round and round in circles and can't seem to break out of a particular loop, the forces of satanic delay and denial may have been projected against you.

In productive patience, you go through a normal process of growth, development, and maturity before manifestation. For example, no matter how you pray, fast and declare over a pregnant woman, she still has to wait nine months before delivering her child. Your prayers can only protect her, not cancel the process of waiting for nine months.

You can't change a divine process that God has instituted. You can't pray it forward or downward. You'll have to wait through that process. That normal process of waiting in the divine process is what I call productive patience. That's what divine delays represent.

God knows I love my five-year-old boy, Isaac. Unfortunately, I can't give him the car to drive right now. Many times, he has cried for it, but I can't allow him. Yes, I do love him, but he has to grow and become an adult, then learn to drive before I can allow him to drive. For now, let him continue with the toys.

Are you getting the picture?

> Understanding productive patience is vital so that we can separate demonic delays from time of the normal growth process.

In productive patience or divine delays, there are apparent processes of growth and development that you're going through. You're not where you're supposed to be, but you're making gradual progress towards the bigger dreams. Every day and every year is a plus on the previous.

But in demonic delays, you're just stagnated. You could feel the frustration and palpable sense of *"something is wrong somewhere. This is not where I'm supposed to be."*

UNDERSTANDING SATANIC DELAYS

The truth is that anyone who has ever tried to live by faith has experienced delays. Not everything has happened in the time frame we wanted them. This is a fact no one can deny.

But the truth is that not all delays are God-programmed. Most delays are satanic and can lead to denial. They are programmed by the devil to lead to discouragement and ultimately to backsliding.

Most delays are part of the spiritual conflict we face as Christians. They are nothing else than spiritual attacks projected to stop us from manifesting the plans of God and His blessings for our lives.

> Satanic delays and denial are times of extreme frustration, when one's blessings are prevented from manifesting despite so much efforts and labor. This leads to loss of faith and many questions in the hearts of the victims.

I believe this was what the wise man meant in Proverbs 13:12 when he said, *"Hope deferred maketh the heart sick: but when the desire cometh, it is a tree of life."* The Good News Translation renders that verse this way: *"When hope is crushed, the heart is crushed, but a wish come true fills you with joy."*

I doubt anyone will say that God likes to crush people's heart. On the contrary, we know that God is the One who fills us with joy. This also means that it is not God who crushes our hope so that He can break our hearts. It is the devil. The devil does that through the force of delays and denial.

DANIEL AND THE PRINCE OF PERSIA

Daniel chapter ten gives an unambiguous picture of the invisible struggle between the forces of good and evil. Daniel had prayed, and an angel was dispatched to bring his request from the very first day he began praying. But a demon referred to as the *prince of Persia* waylaid the angel and engaged him in intense spiritual warfare.

Imagine that.

That's like a monitoring spirit, an evil spirit in charge of that area. This evil spirit's mission was to delay and deny Daniel answers to his prayers.

How many times have we faced delays and even outright denials that we attribute it to the making of God, when in reality, they were the making of demonic powers?

If Daniel had stopped praying on the 10th day of his petition, he probably might not have received the answer to his prayer. His persistence in prayer empowered his spiritual victory over the forces projected to delay, stop or deny his prayers.

Here's the point:

> *Demonic delays are aimed at denying you answers to your prayers. That's when delays can become denials.*

I have said many times that God has given us all things that pertain to life and godliness (2 Peter 1:3)...Your future husband is not in heaven. He's here on earth. If he's not coming forth physically, you need to learn how to command him to manifest.

Your money is not in heaven. Not at all. There are no dollars and pounds and rands in heaven. All the monies you'll ever need are here on earth. If you're always getting frustrated financially, you need to learn how to command your finances to manifest.

If you've been in the same spot for a very long time, that's not God. The forces of delay and denial are responsible. Gather yourself up and begin to release prayer bullets against these powers.

Deliverance by Fire

JACOB AND LABAN

In Genesis chapter 29, Jacob set out to marry Rachel, the love of his life. He didn't have money to pay the bride price, so he chose to labor seven years instead. That is commendable. How many men would do that today?

Unfortunately, at the end of the agreed seven years, he was cheated out of his dream. He was outwitted. So, he had to labor an extra seven years again.

It sounds easy when we read and retell that story, but Jacob will tell you that those were some of the most difficult and frustrating times of his life. Can you imagine serving as a slave for fourteen years just to get married to a woman you love? Something that was to take seven years eventually took fourteen years. Something was not right there. The forces of delay and denial were at work through Laban against Jacob.

> Some people have worked so hard all their lives in a company, but when it's time for them to get a benefit, one problem or the other crops up. They end up losing the blessing.

I know a minister of the Gospel who labored in a Church for 20 years plus. Just when it was time for him to retire and earn his entitlements, something happened, and he was suspended, and later dismissed from the church. When we sat down and discussed the situation with him, it was apparent the devil did that because there was no concrete reason he should be treated that way.

> **When you're working so hard and getting so little results, beloved, the forces of delay and denial are working against your life.**

When you're due for a promotion, and you're not promoted, instead others get promoted while you have to make do with what is available, dear friend, begin to bind the powers of delay and denial from now onwards.

PAUL AND SATAN

For we wanted to come to you– yes I, Paul, did, again and again–but Satan blocked our way (1 Thessalonians 2:18).

Wait a minute. How's that? Did you see that?

Satan blocked Paul! Great Paul!

Paul knew what he wanted to do was God's will. He had that witness in his heart, but Satan raised several oppositions and blocked him, and Satan did that not even once.

That's amazing, but the undeniable truth.

If there's a dream in your heart that you know is God's perfect will for your life. And you have this peace that it's time to birth it, but the more you try, the more you're prevented, arise and begin to come against the forces of delay and denial.

Many people are stuck at one spot today and have lost the courage to venture out again to start their dreams because they have faced so many disappointments that they wonder if they were right in the first place. My friend, the forces of delay and denial is what is working against you. Get back and go on the offensive against these powers, and then move into God's dream for your life.

DELAYED FOR 38 YEARS

In John chapter 5, we read the story of a man who stayed in one spot for 38 years. He was at the pool of mercy but didn't obtain mercy for so many years. The devil so worked against this man that people hated him even in his helpless state.

Have you asked yourself how it is possible that this man could be there for 38 years and no one deemed it fit to give him some assistance? There was no one, not even a family member, a passerby, an observer, or some good person out there to assist him. How's that?

The devil.

He was a victim of the forces of delay and denial.

> The forces of delay and denial can so work against a person that he will be helpless even in the midst of plenty opportunities flying around him. People will just hate him for no just cause. He will lack help and support and be so alone in his struggles.

There are many more examples of people who were victims of the powers of delay and denial. But the good news is that God intervened eventually, and the story changed.

But you have to recognize this problem and begin to resist it today.

CAUSES OF DEMONIC DELAYS

1. Habitual Sin: You're a Christian, but there's this sin you can't just let go. Your spirit is always convicting you of it, but you just can't get over it. Beloved, yes, God is a merciful God. The Blood of Jesus Christ is speaking mercy and forgiveness, always.

But habitual sin opens a gate for the enemy to be able to create obstructions in your life. It's time to pray and deal with this habitual sin.

2. Disobedience to Divine Instruction: We can also open doors to spiritual delays when we are disobedient to divine instructions. That is, there are things that God is putting in your heart to do, but you're too busy with other things not to mind. This will undoubtedly cause you to experience a lot of delays in life.

3. Lack of Personal Development: I was praying with a sister the other day, and she said: *"I'm experiencing some kind of hate in my office, from my seniors to my colleagues. They rarely talk to me. But somehow, they can't get rid of me because they know they can't do much without me."*

That's excellent. You're just too useful that the enemy can't let you go.

The Bible encourages us to develop virtues of creativity, love, and sound mind. It is not the will of God for Christians to be liabilities or second classes. We are to become so good at what we do that we are the light where we are.

4. When You're Out of God's Will: Do you remember Naomi and his family? (Ruth 1) They left the country when there was famine. Unfortunately, this was not God's will for their lives. The hunger in their land was only temporary. But they were too consumed with what they wanted and didn't pay attention to what God needed them to do at the moment. Well, the family lost almost everything.

Many believers, either out of omission or commission, have stepped out of God's will for their lives and are chasing fantasies today; hence, they are being buffeted by the forces of darkness like never before.

One prayer to pray with every seriousness today is this:

> *"O LORD, forgive me in any way I have stepped out of your will for my life. Have mercy on me and restore me to Your will once again, in Jesus name."*

5. Witchcraft: No doubt, witchcraft spirits can also create delays and denials for many people. On Day 9 we talked about this and provided prayers against witchcraft.

The truth is that there are many people suffering one form of delay or the other today because of witchcraft manipulations against them. I wish this was something I could just wish away. But it's not. It's real.

6. Curses: Curses can also be responsible for spiritual delays.

What are curses? What are the different types of curses? How do I know if I'm under a curse? What should I do if I discover I'm a victim of curses? All these questions are answered in another section of this book.

7. Past Evil Covenants, Soul Ties, and Unholy Alliances: These include childhood initiations and dedications to spirits, blood covenants, unholy agreements and oaths, bathing in the river rituals, love oaths, seeking a solution from diviners, etc.

All of these have the power to invoke the powers of delay and denial against a person. Honest repentance and renouncement of these acts is the way to break free from the problems they've created.

8. Charismatic Witchcraft: Many genuine believers are suffering one problem or the other today, including delays and denials, because they've had hands laid on them by evil people who put on the cloth of men and women of God, but are actually wolves in sheep clothing. That is why the Bible warns us against running up and down seeking miracles and prophecies.

The devil is capitalizing on the age of prophecy and also empowering people who go about initiating people instead of setting them free.

Make no mistake about this: Evil hands laid on you can also produce the effects of witchcraft in your life.

9. Modern Spiritism: Such as astrology, reading and working with the zodiac signs, tarot cards, magic, etc. These are all forms of demonic activities condemned in the Bible. Involvement in these practices will ultimately lead to one form of eventual satanic stronghold or the other.

10. Higher Degrees of Satanic Attack: There are other forms of demonic delays and coordinated attacks that can produce spiritual delays and even denials, different from curses and witchcraft manipulations. The types of attacks that Paul and Daniel had were not curses or witchcraft manipulations. They were a higher level of demonic operations. These types of operations are mainly targeted at stopping God's assignment. They are perpetrated by principalities and powers and geared towards stopping the entrance of the gospel.

Ministers need to be able to discern when their works for God are being targeted by the devil and engage in prolonged spiritual warfare to break the powers of delay and denial.

HOW TO BREAK THE POWERS OF DELAY AND DENIAL

Howbeit this kind goeth not out but by prayer and fasting (Matthew 17:21).

Jesus recognized that some demonic activities cannot break or leave except through prayer and fasting. I wish there were other ways. But the good news is that no demonic activity is impossible to break. In the name of Jesus Christ, every knee will bow and all powers submit.

Are you currently going through some experiences you believe are a manifestation of the powers of delay and denial?

Then brace up. They can be broken, and you can obtain your victory in Christ. Here are the steps you must follow…

- Genuine repentance and honest renunciation of habitual sin

- If possible, get someone to pray a prayer of agreement with you for a few days

- Locate anything that might be giving the devil a doorway into your life and deal with it.

- Renounce all covenants, curses, agreements and unholy alliances of the past that is still speaking against you.

- Anoint yourself and dedicate your life to Christ.

PRAYERS

Instruction

- Pray these prayers in the midnight for several days, in addition to other prayers.

- Write your name, your partner's name, and your family members names on a plain paper. Then begin this prayer to rebuke the spirit of delay and stagnation.

- List the particular areas of life that you are experiencing a delay, and begin to reverse it

……

Prayers

Heavenly Father, I thank You for the opportunity to appear before You once again to obtain mercy and find help in times of need. Be glorified in Jesus name.

O Lord, I pray, if the delay in my life right now is caused by me, by my disobedience, laziness, walking out of your will, or attitudes, please forgive me and restore me in Jesus name.

Deliverance by Fire

Father Lord, if the delays in my life are from You, open my eyes to see what You want me to see, my ears to hear what you want me to understand, and my understanding to learn what You want me to learn, in Jesus name.

Father Lord, I am rejecting all forms of demonic delays in my life and family today. I nullify every curse or evil projection producing frustrating delays in my life and the lives all these names here..........in the name of Jesus Christ.

I delist my name and the names in this paper right now **(mention the names)** from every list used to project delays and stagnation in our lives, in Jesus name

---

Father, Lord, You are my help and my deliverer; You are the hope of the afflicted and the needy; O Lord, please do not delay again in my --------- (mention the area you are experiencing delays). Send me help speedily, in Jesus name.

Today, O Lord, I speak to everything that has made any area of my life dormant, as Jesus addressed the barren fig tree, I speak to them now to be withered from their root, in Jesus name.

All you powers of delay and denial against my life and family, seize today, in Jesus name.

O Lord, anoint me with the power to pursue, overtake and recover my stolen properties from the power of delay.

I silence every false prophet speaking against my advancement, and bring to naught all evil counselors and counsels against my breakthrough, in the name of Jesus.

My miracles and breakthrough shall no longer tarry. My expectations shall no longer delay. By the power of God, I command them to start speaking and manifesting from this day forward, in Jesus name

---

Every arrow of disappointment and shame fired against my destiny, my marriage, my family, my career, and my purpose in life, backfire, in the name of Jesus Christ.

Deliverance by Fire

Henceforth, I overcome the powers of carelessness, laziness, and procrastination. I overcome every attitude in my life working against my progress. I decree that these little foxes that have eaten deep into my life and family are destroyed from today, in the name of Jesus Christ.

Whatever is responsible for my working hard and earning little, I end it today by fire in the name of Jesus Christ.

I at this moment reverse all forms of demonic delay in the following areas of my life:

....

I decree supernatural restoration and speed in these areas, in Jesus name.

According to the book of **Isaiah 65:20-24**, *I decree:*

"Never again will there be an infant who lives but a few days in my family, or an old man who does not live out his years; even at a hundred, we will be thought to be mere children.

We will build houses and dwell in them; we will plant vineyards and eat their fruit. No longer will we build homes and others live in them, or plant and others eat.

For as the days of a tree, so will be my days and the days of every one I call out their names right now.

(Mention the names on your list)

We will enjoy the works of our hands. We will not labor in vain, nor bring forth children doomed to misfortune.

The Lord will bless us, we and our descendants,

In Jesus name.

FOR FURTHER READING

Daniel 10, John 5

Day 12: Dealing With the Spirits of Infirmity

₁₀Now He was teaching in one of the synagogues on the Sabbath. 11 And behold, there was a woman who had a spirit of infirmity eighteen years, and was bent over and could in no way raise herself up.

₁₂But when Jesus saw her, He called her to Him and said to her, **"Woman, you are loosed from your infirmity."** ₁₃And He laid His hands on her, and immediately she was made straight and glorified God.

₁₄But the ruler of the synagogue answered with indignation because Jesus had healed on the Sabbath; and he said to the crowd, "There are six days on which men ought to work; therefore come and be healed on them, and not on the Sabbath day."

₁₅The Lord then answered him and said, "Hypocrite! Does not each one of you on the Sabbath loose his ox or donkey from the stall, and lead it away to water *it?* ₁₆*So ought not this woman, being a daughter of Abraham, whom Satan has bound—think of it—for eighteen years, be loosed from this bond on the Sabbath?"* ₁₇*And when He said these things, all His adversaries were put to shame; and all the multitude rejoiced for all the glorious things that were done by Him* – **Luke 13:10-17.**

Jesus understood the reality of the spiritual conflict between man and satan. His ministry on earth was about stopping these evil works of the devil in every way. He spoke to evil spirits with authority, destroyed their activities and commanded them to leave, and they obeyed. He set the captives free.

In fact, Jesus is unhappy when the church doesn't discern the works of the devil and set the captives free. Just like the woman in this story, some people can be in church for many years, be faithful in church attendance and may even be workers in the church, but have demons afflict them and keep them in suffering. Until the demons are commanded to leave, they'll stay.

> **You can't wish away problems caused by demons. You can't resolve problems caused by demons by motivational speeches or long religious talks. You deal with them by discerning them and commanding them to seize, in Jesus name.**

The spirits of infirmity caused this woman to be bowed. Doctors today would have explained to her that she had Multiple sclerosis, a potentially disabling disease of the brain and spinal cord. They would have told her that *"it is a situation where the immune system attacks the defensive sheath (myelin) that covers nerve fibers and causes communication glitches between your brain and the rest of your body. Eventually, the disease can cause the nerves themselves to worsen or become permanently damaged."* Then they would have advised her that there's no cure for multiple sclerosis. That treatment can only modify the course of the disease and manage symptoms.

Fortunately, Jesus saw that it was a demon or demons that was behind this situation and prayed for her healing by commanding the demons to go. How many people today have accepted certain conditions as something they would need to live with and manage based on a medical recommendation, while they are situations caused by demons.

From this story, we see that demons can be responsible for specific health conditions. It was the demons that made her crippled, or unable to walk without assistance for eighteen long years.

The word used as ***infirmity*** in the above passage is the same word used in Romans 8:26 (KJV). It is the same Greek word that means a weakness of the physical body or the soul. That is, a weakness of the body or the mind.

> So the spirits of infirmity attack the physical body or the mind and bring weakness to it, making it unable to function normally, or keeping it in constant pain.

We know that we cannot blame every illness or every emotional problem on demons. There may be a number of reasons a person may be struggling with sickness or emotional issue. It can be a result of genetics, environments, food, lack of exercise, etc. But some of the problems can be caused by demons. In fact, the percentage of illnesses caused by demons may be higher than we know.

In Mark Chapter 5 we read the story of the woman with the issue of blood. The Bible says *"She had suffered a great deal under the care of many doctors and had spent all she had, yet instead of getting better she grew worse"* (Vs. 26). While the Bible didn't mention the spirits of infirmity here, it gives us a clear picture that this woman's situation was the work of demons. She had tried doctor after doctor, treatment after treatment, test after test, scan after scan, but she got worse. The doctors couldn't help.

> **When health and emotional situations are a work of demons, they defy medical help.**

A sister wrote, *"I have been struggling with severe fibromyalgia, fatigue, and nervous system problems since my second daughter was born six years ago. Doctors cannot find what's wrong with me on tests. And it is so debilitating. I want to be free from this persistent pain and illness."*

No doubt, that's the spirit of infirmity.

The spirits of infirmity afflict people in two ways:

1. Causing physical health problems

According to our text, these demons of infirmity made this woman bowed, unable to walk without aid. She was in pain and tension for eighteen years. That's long enough, don't you think so?

If you or somebody you know is struggling with health problems that you've tried to get medical help from, but to no avail, then the spirits of infirmity may be responsible for the situation. If these demons could create a case of disability, then don't think they won't attempt to create other issues. It's time to pray against these demons with authority.

2. Causing emotional disorder

The demons of infirmity can also produce depression, anxiety, hopelessness, self-pity, self-condemnation, life-threatening inferiority complex, and other emotional attacks. The goal is to keep their victims bowed and down, and unable to live a normal life.

If you've been struggling with an anxiety disorder, depression, and other mental problems, and medical solutions seem not be helping, you may be under the attack of demons of infirmity. Bring these situations before the Blood of Jesus Christ and reject the demons causing them.

Open Doors for the Demons of Infirmity

How do the demons of infirmity gain access to a person's life?

=> **Childhood abuse:** if you were abused as a child, it could create a situation of pain in you that the spirits of infirmity can exploit to gain access into your life.

=> **Trauma:** if you had a traumatic experience in the past that you haven't opened up to the Lord for complete healing and restoration, it could give the demons of infirmity a foothold in your life.

=> **Unresolved offenses** that create bitterness in the heart, unforgiveness, anger, and desire for vengeance.

=> **Evil dreams:** a sister was in the dream and ate human flesh. When she woke up, she started having rashes all over her body. All treatments failed until she began to pray and rebuke the demons of infirmity in prayers

=> **Addiction:** If you're addicted to alcohol, drugs, overeating, demonic movies that promote witchcraft, vampire, etc. they can be an open door for the demons of infirmity to attack your body or mind and bring weakness and pain.

=> **Refer above:** on day two, we talked about several things that can serve as an open door for demons into a person's life. Examine yourself and come before the Lord with an open heart for help.

As we saw in the woman's case:

- She was not born deformed. A demon caused her deformity.

- She tried to get cure from physicians, but their treatments didn't help.

- She would have died in her pain if Jesus didn't set her free with authoritative prayers and decree.

- Demons don't show mercy to their victims. They can stay for as long as they can, unless they are rebuked, in Jesus name.

Our focus today is to stand in prayers against the demons of infirmity. If you don't have these problems, then come to the Lord in prayers on behalf of your loved ones, or other people you know who may be having health problems that several medical diagnoses have failed to help.

PRAYERS

Instruction

Today, you're going to pray for yourself and for those you know who are suffering in their health. So write out the names of those you will be praying for.

You can pray today's prayers any time, not necessarily in the midnight.

Prayers

1. Thank God for it is His will to heal you and your loved ones.

2. Ask God to reveal to you and the people you're praying for what might be the doorway for the demons of infirmity to operate.

3. Based on what the Lord is inspiring you, plead the Blood of Jesus Christ over the foundation and sources of the spirits of infirmity.

4. Mention the specific health problems you're going through and command the demons responsible for them to leave in the name of Jesus Christ.

5. Decree: *Father, in the name of Jesus Christ, I overcome every spirit of infirmity in my life and family from this day forward, in Jesus name.*

6. Decree: *Jesus died for our freedom. He shed His Blood for our salvation and healing. I, therefore, declare every attack on my health and the health of .... illegal. I curse these unlawful activities against our health to end today, in Jesus name.*

7. Pray: *Heavenly Father, deliver me from every buried hurt, anger and bitterness in my life, in Jesus name.*

8. Decree: *From today forward, I make my spirit, soul, and body a Holy place for the Lord and the Spirit of God. It will no longer be a house for all demons of infirmity, in Jesus name.*

9. Decree: *Every demon of infirmity causing me to be sick, bowed, in pain, and in mental torment, pack your loads right now and depart. I cast you all into the abyss in the name of Jesus Christ.*

10. Decree: *In the Mighty name of Jesus Christ, I disconnect myself and .... from all forms of evil covenants that the demons of infirmity are using as a legal ground to attack our bodies, in Jesus name.*

11. Command: *Fire from heaven, destroy every evil deposit in my life, and the lives of .... causing sickness, depression, sorrow, and continuous pain, in Jesus name.*

12. Anoint yourself and the names you've written out and declare that your bodies are henceforth the temples of the Holy Spirit, sanctified for God's use only, in Jesus name.

10. Take the Holy Communion and decree that You are connected to God's covenant of life through the Blood of Jesus

Christ. Therefore, whatever could not stop the death and resurrection of Christ cannot stop the freedom You now have and enjoy.

11. Thank God for total deliverance from the spirits of infirmity, in Jesus name.

Amen.

FOR FURTHER READING

Luke 13 and 18

Day 13: Praying Against the Forces of Injustice

Evil men do not understand justice, but those who seek the Lord understand it completely. - Proverbs 28:5

I started praying against the forces and demons of injustice after reading two stories that touched my heart so much. Here are excerpts of the two stories. You can Google and read their details online.

Story 1: For rushing neighbor to the hospital, man spends two years in prison

A man was jailed for two years after he volunteered to take his sick neighbor, who later died, to the hospital. He was accused of murder by the deceased's family members. The man identified as Mr. Chidiebere Onwumere, a native of Umuagbaghagha village in Osisioma local government area of Abia state, only got to be released after the intervention of a legal practitioner, Barr. Uzosike.

Narrating his ordeal to Abia Facts Newspaper after his release from Nigerian prisons in Afara, Umuahia on Tuesday, Mr Chidiebere who was full of praises to God for

Deliverance by Fire

vindicating him after two years of suffering for a crime he knew nothing about, said it was in his bid to save a neighbor that caused him to experience this injustice.

Story 2: Innocent man demands £1m compensation after spending 17 years in jail for lookalike's crime

An innocent man who spent 17 years in jail for a crime he did not commit is seeking nearly £1million compensation after police found his criminal lookalike. Richard Jones, from Kansas City, was released last year after a judge called into question his original conviction.

....

Look at these stories. It's easy to scroll past stuff like that especially when one is not directly involved. But can you imagine the torture and pain that these people went through? Can you imagine the trauma and setback that their families experienced? These are just two among millions of cases like these every year.

In my country, for example, there are many such cases. People get mistaken for what they didn't do, and they spend years in jail without any reason. They are victims of the forces of injustice!

I'm sure you know that God is not the one who orchestrated those situations. The devil did, and we know his goal – to steal, kill and destroy.

> *Therefore the Lord will wait, that He may be gracious to you; and therefore He will be exalted, that He may have mercy on you. For* **the Lord is a God of justice**; *blessed are all those who wait for Him.* - Isaiah 30:18

God is a God of justice. He also commands us to be people of justice. Conversely, Satan is the planner, deviser, and orchestrator of injustice. Injustice is one way he tries to terminate people's destiny and stop them from becoming who God wants them to be. I can't imagine how many people's futures and life purposes have been destroyed by the forces and demons of injustice.

Injustice is unfairness, discrimination, bias in judgment against someone. It is taking what belongs to others and claiming right on top of that. It is exploiting others without fear of any consequences. The demons of injustice are some of the most wicked sets of evil spirits.

Apart from the kinds of stories I shared above, the forces of injustice can also manifest in the following ways:

- Always getting punished for offenses that one did not commit.

- Being falsely accused from time to time.

- Always cheated in a business relationship

- Facing extreme discrimination in life, business and places of work

- Being forced to pay what you did not owe

- People's minds always getting poisoned against you

- Being queried in the workplace for things that another person did

- Not believed when telling the truth of how something happened, and getting punished instead, in the place of the offender

- Losing your properties from time to time to unprovoked attacks

- Being a victim of robbery and thievery from time to time.

- Racism and slavery are also a manifestation of the demons of injustice

God didn't say we should fight injustice by power by might. Of course, vengeance belongs to God. But we need to come in prayer against the forces of injustice.

While we may not call down fire on those individuals who the devil is using, we can pray and rebuke the demons using them and claim God's justice in obvious situations. God reserves the right to determine how to carry out judgment. But we must recognize that injustice is not one of His gifts and blessings to us and resist the evil attacks in prayers.

> *Learn to do good; seek justice, correct oppression; bring justice to the fatherless, plead the widow's cause. - Isaiah 1:17*

Apart from speaking out when we can, we can also seek justice and correct oppression through prayers and intercession.

Today, I call you to take a moment to pray against the forces of injustice and claim God's justice in your family, and that of your loved ones.

PRAYERS

Dear Heavenly Father, I thank You because You are a God of justice. You will never forsake Your people. You preserve us always and keep our soul from harm. May Your name be glorified in Jesus name.

Father, I pray today that You thwart all forms of injustice meted out against me and my family members in the past and bring us justice, in Jesus name.

I pray, Lord, may all evil agents of injustice projected against my life and destiny lose their strength and seize operation in Jesus name.

O Lord, I speak against every decision and unjust judgments that have been decided against my family and me. I reverse them today in the name of Jesus Christ.

O Lord, I claim restoration in all areas of my life that I have suffered injustice, in the name of Jesus Christ.

O Lord, it is an abomination before You to justify the wicked and condemn the innocent (Proverbs 17:15). I, therefore, pray that all those who are set out to condemn my family and me unjustly be exposed and their plans frustrated, in Jesus name.

O Lord, I overthrow any man or woman sitting on my blessing, promotion, and freedom. I command them to become disabled today, in Jesus name.

I refuse to be judged and condemned henceforth by the ungodly. Even where I have missed it in the past, my confession of sin, repentance and the mercy of Christ is now my boldness.

I at this moment reverse every form of adverse judgment that the ungodly, the devil, and sinners have held and decreed against me. I replace all these contrary agreements with the blessings of God, in Jesus name.

O LORD, the God of vengeance, O God of vengeance, let your glorious justice shine forth, in Jesus name (Psalm 94:1)

Deliverance by Fire

Father Lord, I pray, concerning my marriage, children, finances, home, spouse, and ministry. O Lord, arise and bring us justice today, in Jesus name.

Father, I pray that when I am faced with apparent situations of injustice, empower me with the right words, give me the boldness, and inspire me with ideas on what I need to do to protect the oppressed, in Jesus name.

Dear Lord, I pray for the following persons who have experienced injustice in their lives, and are hurting right now:

....

O Lord, heal them of their hurts and restore them in Jesus name.

Father, Lord, burn down the strongholds of injustice and robbery in our lives and restore unto us everything the enemy has stolen from us through the forces of injustice at work, in the name of Jesus Christ.

Father, Lord, according to Your Word, You love justice, hate robbery and what is wrong (Isaiah 61:8). Therefore, Lord, I pray for justice in the following areas of my life

………………….   ………………….   ………………….

By Your mercy correct every adverse verdict working against me in them this day, and glorify Your name, in Jesus name.

O Lord, empower me to turn away from evil and do good continually; so that I shall dwell in Your presence, always. For You, Lord loves justice, and will not forsake those who seek You, in Jesus name.

FOR FURTHER READING

Luke 18

Day 14: Deliverance from Financial Hardship

Culled from my blog post at www.betterlifeworld.org

But thou shalt remember the LORD thy God: for it is he that gives you the power to get wealth, that he may establish his covenant which he sware unto thy fathers, as it is this day.- Deut. 8:18

Let's start today by making the following declarations:

- "I believe that poverty is not God's will for my life.

- "God delights in my prosperity.

- "I am a seed of Abraham, Isaac, and Jacob, through Jesus Christ.

- "Today, I am receiving the power and wisdom to create wealth, in Jesus name. Amen."

Our website receives over 200 prayer requests monthly. Many of these prayer requests bother on finance - debt, job, rent, urgent financial needs, need for miraculous supply, and so on. There are usually very aching stories around these requests.

And one thing I've discerned from these requests and my personal experience is that, many times, the problem is not because the persons involved are not making efforts physically. Sometimes the people are doing all they can, but something is not just connecting; other times you could see that there's some spiritual chain or burden on the person's finances.

Do you remember the story of Peter in Luke chapter 5? Verse 5 says, *"But Simon answered and said to Him, 'Master, we have toiled all night and caught nothing; nevertheless at Your word, I will let down the net.'"*

Every professional fisher knows that the night hours are the best times to go fishing. So Peter didn't sleep off or go clubbing and expect manna from above in the morning. He was up and doing as long as his profession was concerned. But despite all his hard work, he caught nothing.

> There are times that one is doing their best, but like Peter, are not catching anything at the end of everything. They keep toiling and toiling and nothing to show for it.

May I say to you today: If you're currently going through a financial crisis, God can give you stability. God can deliver you and give you great supernatural breakthrough. He can give you a better job; He can inspire a raise for you; He can cause your debtors to pay, and He can bless your business. It won't take anything to give you relief from your financial predicament – it doesn't matter how stubborn the situation seems.

But like Peter, you need to pay attention to God's ideas and inspirations in your heart going forward. At Christ's instruction, Peter's all-night frustration ended like in a dream. If you can calm down and discern God's voice regarding your present financial problem, your deliverance is settled. I've not seen a financial problem so big enough to withstand God's revelational direction.

Before we proceed, pray like this:

Heavenly Father, I know that all things are possible with You. There is no situation too difficult before You. Yes, I may be feeling pressured and cornered in my financial life at the moment, but it doesn't stop the fact that this situation is nothing before You. I praise You in advance for my deliverance and breakthrough. And I pray that You give me clear insight and direction on what to do, where to go, who to connect with, as I seek You, in Jesus name.

There are times that you have to look up to God for a new word, a new direction, and a new idea to deal with your financial problems. Don't forget that.

Praying Against Financial Demons

Financial demons are evil spirits that are working very hard to frustrate your finances. They will stop at nothing until they are sure you're completely zeroed. They can create what I call *the Assyrian Attack*. Let me show you that in the Scriptures:

> And it happened after this that Ben-Hadad king of Syria gathered all his army, and went up and besieged Samaria. And there was a great famine in Samaria, and indeed they besieged it until a donkey's head was sold for eighty shekels of silver, and one-fourth of a kab of dove droppings for five shekels of silver. - 2 Kings 6:24-25

Please read that scripture again. Notice that God didn't create that scarcity and problem. Let's reread it from a more Modern Bible Translation:

After this happened, King Ben-Hadad of Aram gathered all his army and went to surround and attack the city of Samaria. The soldiers would not let people bring food into the city, **so there was a time of terrible hunger in Samaria. It was so bad in Samaria that a donkey's head was sold for 80 pieces of silver and one pint of dove's dung sold for five pieces of silver**.*-(ERV)*

Benhadad, who is a representation of the devil, built a siege on Samaria that led to food prices soaring astronomically. It got so bad that a donkey's head was sold for fifty dollars and a pint of dove's dung for about three dollars. In fact, in 2 Kings 6:28-30, the situation got terribly bad that people began to eat their children to survive, all because of the siege built by the enemy.

A siege is a barrier, an obstruction, a barricade, a restriction, a hindrance, a difficulty, a limitation, or something just preventing you from getting through to your desire and connecting with your breakthrough. If you've seen where police created a barrier in a crime scene to stop people for trespassing, that's precisely how a siege is. It creates a barrier that prevents a person from reaching their desired points.

In the Bible days, sieges were usually used in military invasions and warfare. When an army attacks a city and wants the occupants to surrender willfully, they apply a military strategy called **laying a siege**. They build a fortress or cordon over the city or country, cutting off food, water, communication and then send a message to the city to surrender. An invading army whose aim is to force the citizens of a city to effortless submission smartly and strategically surrounds the city, cuts off food, water, communication, and transportation into the city and then demands that the inhabitants surrender themselves willfully.

There are three combinations of actions usually perpetrated by a siege. They are:

- Restriction of food provisions resulting in death by starvation.

- Restriction of water supply resulting in death from dehydration.

- Restriction of communication and transportation between neighboring cities and their fresh troops, thus creating a communication gap, lack of access to help, and strategic information regarding what's happening.

That is precisely the tactic the devil has employed in his war against countless believers and their finances. He creates a fence around them, first cutting them off from food (the Word of God), water (the Holy Spirit), and communication (the Rhema voice of God). He then and then unleashes severe hardship, famine, spiritual attacks, nightmares, evil dreams, illnesses, depression, and hatred, against the person.

Here's the point:

Don't let the devil take you away from the word of God and prayers when you have financial problems.

The devil makes people believe that they do not need God to solve money problems. But that's a lie. One idea, revelation, Rhema, inspiration or direction from God will put to an end a lifetime of struggles.

Here are signs that your finances may be under a siege:

- You're currently going through some severe financial famine;

- You're working so hard, but after all said and done, there's not much to show for it.

- You desperately want to find a job, and you're doing the best you can, but it's not forthcoming

- Any time a major financial blessing is coming your way, something just happens, and you lose it.

- When you're due for promotion, you don't get it, even when others who are less qualified get theirs

- You experience extreme disfavor in the workplace; no one wants to help you

- People willfully owe you money and never want to pay, even though they have it

- You can't normally explain how you spend money. You just feel that money comes, but it just runs away

- You're stuck in some place in life, business, and career. Stagnant and not making gradual progress.

- You work for people, and they never want to pay you. You have to always struggle to get paid for what you have worked for

- You are always struggling financially

- You have this feeling that something is wrong somewhere.

- You're never out of debt. Before you receive some breakthrough, issues have piled up so much that before the money comes, it's already spent. Thus, you're forced always to continue to struggle.

- etc

Today, arise and begin to command the sieges, financial demons and barriers against your finances to seize.

PRAYERS

Prophetic Declarations

1. *Father, in the name of Jesus Christ, I declare according to Psalm 35:27 and 3 John 1:2 that it is the will of God for me to prosper and be in good health. God delights in my prosperity. Not in my lack.*

Therefore, today, I shout for joy. I sing praise and dance before God. I magnify His name because He is causing me to prosper and excel. The demons of lack, debt, scarcity, and frustration have lost in my life and family, in Jesus name.

---

2. *It is written in Luke chapter 6:38 that if I give, it shall be given unto you; good measure, pressed down, shaken together, and running over, shall men give into my bosom. For with the same degree that I give withal it shall be measured to me again.*

I, therefore, decree that all my seeds and giving in the past are not in vain. And I shall not give up on giving. From today, Lord, I declare that men and

women will have the desire and joy to bless me. I decree that the hearts of men will work in my favor, in Jesus name.

---

3. According to Philippians 4:19, God shall supply all my needs according to His riches in glory by Christ Jesus. And according to 2 Corinthians 9:8 - God can make all grace abound toward me; that I, always having all sufficiency in all things, may abound to every good work.

I, therefore, declare today that I shall not be in lack. God's riches in Christ are providing my needs. His grace abounds towards me. I have all sufficiency and abound in every good work, in Jesus name

---

4. It is written in Psalms 1:3 that the righteous shall be like a tree planted by the rivers of water, that brings his fruit in his season; his leaf also shall not wither, and whatsoever he doeth shall prosper.

I do not walk in the counsel of the ungodly, nor sit in the sit of the scornful. My delight is in the law of God. Therefore, I am like a tree planted by the rivers of water. I am bringing forth my fruits in my season.

My hands are blessed. Whatever I do is prospering henceforth, in Jesus name.

PRAYER 1 – SURRENDER

Once again, O Lord, I thank You for it is Your will that I should walk in prosperity. Your plans for my life does not include frustration and financial crisis from time to time. For this I say, thank You, Lord, in Jesus name.

Lord, sometimes I assume that prosperity, money, and wealth are by my efforts alone. LORD, I come to YOU this day and confess my ignorance and pride. Forgive me for not giving YOU the ultimate place in my finances in the past. Have mercy on me for the sake of the Blood of Jesus Christ, in Jesus name.

Lord, I bring before you every attitude in me that led to my financial scarcity. I take responsibility today and ask for forgiveness. Forgive me for all my poor financial choices, wrong investment decisions, lack of savings, comparing myself with others in shopping, living above my means. Father, forgive and have mercy on me, in Jesus name.

I thank YOU, LORD Jesus because in You I have forgiveness of sins. In YOU I have the grace to appear before the Almighty God to obtain mercy and find grace in time of need. In YOU I have the assurance that as I pray, I receive answers. Thank You for bringing me before God through Your blood for help in my financial situation today, in Jesus name.

PRAYER 2 – POWER TO OBEY

Heavenly Father, it is written in Job 36:11, that if I obey and serve YOU, that I will spend my days in prosperity and my years in plenty. Lord, I ask You to baptize me with zeal to obey Your Word on finances henceforth. Give me the grace to be a doer of Your Word and not a hearer alone, in Jesus name.

Deliverance by Fire

Holy Spirit, please make me willing and obedient to the WORD of God from this day forward so that I may eat the good things of the land, in Jesus name.

Let every seed of financial greed and disobedience be uprooted from my life today by fire, in Jesus name.

O Lord, make me a blessing in this world, that my life will be a light and support to those who are in need, for it is written that when I give, You will command men to give back to me. Inspire me to give and to give joyfully without regrets from today, in Jesus name.

I pray, Holy Spirit, motivate me to honor the Lord with my resources and finances from this day forward, so that my barns will be full and overflowing with harvest... for it is written in Proverbs 3:9-10:

Honor the LORD from your wealth And the first of all your produce; So your barns will be filled with plenty, and your vats will overflow with new wine. In Jesus name

PRAYER 3 – REBUKE THE DEVIL

Heavenly Father, I stand in authority in the name of Jesus Christ right today: I command every demon working against my business, my career and my finances to collapse, be bound and cast into the abyss, in Jesus name.

It is written in Matthew 16:19 that whatsoever I bind here on earth is bound in heaven, and whatsoever I loose here on earth is loosed in heaven. I, therefore, bind every spirit of poverty, lack, frustration, and loss. I cast them into the abyss from today, in Jesus name.

I speak to you, satan, in the name of Jesus Christ, I command you to take your hands off my finances right now in the Name of Jesus.

I speak to the mountain of lack and want; I command them to be removed and cast into the sea from this day, in the Name of Jesus Christ.

I declare all curses against my life and finances null, void, and destroyed from today. I am redeemed from the curse of poverty! I am free from oppression, in the name of Jesus Christ.

I now loose the abundance of God, and all that rightfully belongs to me to start locating me, in Jesus name.

I thank You O Lord that You have a plan for me to overcome this lack and have abundance. I cast all my cares and money worries over on You Lord. I declare that I will not worry anymore, neither will I fret. I have peace, and I'm enjoying God's supplies, in Jesus name.

It is written that angels are ministering spirits sent to minister unto the heirs of salvation. Therefore, LORD, I ask that Your angels of goodness, love, and success begin to minister to my needs henceforth, in the name of Jesus Christ.

Wherever my finances are, whoever is connected to my financial breakthroughs, O LORD, let your angels begin to reconnect them to me this day.

As I step out to work from today, LORD, may men and women bring me favor. May those who owe me pay me. May those I apply to for job accept me and help me. May I be established financially, in Jesus name.

PRAYER 4 –DIVINE IDEAS AND DIRECTION

Heavenly Father, it is written that You give us the power to create wealth. Therefore, I ask You to give me the power, wisdom, and guidance to create wealth in my life, in Jesus name.

LORD, I ask You today for ideas; I ask You for inspiration and divine strategies to turn my career around and grow my business into a global brand. Show me secrets hidden from men and help me to unleash Your full potential in my present endeavor, in Jesus name.

LORD, make me an employer of labor, so that I will be a blessing to others and fulfill the covenant of Abraham which I *inherit in Christ Jesus. Direct me to men and materials that YOU assigned to bring me into my place of financial power before the world began, in Jesus name.*

Holy Spirit, You are my teacher. I ask You to teach me how to make profit. Teach me to become a shining light in my career. Open my eyes to the right job opportunities and profitable business ventures, in Jesus name.

DECLARATIONS

Father, Lord, Your Word says in Psalm 1:3 that I am like a tree planted by the riverside. Therefore, I decree that whatever I do prospers from this day forward, in Jesus name.

It is written in Psalm 112:3 that wealth and riches will be in my house, and his righteousness endures forever. So I decree that my house shall be filled with wealth and riches in Jesus name

God is opening the windows of heaven for me, and meeting my every need according to His riches in glory by Jesus Christ. He is causing men to give unto me good measure, pressed down, shaken together and running over. He has given me the power to create wealth and be a blessing to others.

I'm blessed in the field. I'm blessed going in and going out. I have the favor of God. Favor, breakthrough, success, money and every good thing comes to me from this day forward, in Jesus name.

Thank You, Father, thank You Jesus, and thank You Holy Spirit. Together we are creating wealth and lifting men out of lack and want, in Jesus name I pray.

Amen.

FOR FURTHER READING

Luke 5 and 6, Ephesians 4

Day 15: War Against Anti-Marriage Spirits

Culled from my blog post at www.Betterlifeworld.org

Then God blessed them and said, "Be fruitful and multiply. Fill the earth and govern it. Reign over the fish in the sea, the birds in the sky, and all the animals that scurry along the ground." - Genesis 1:28 (NLT)

You do not need a prophet to tell you that the area we have the harshest attack of the enemy is on the family and marriage front.

Some time ago, after following up on many marriage related issues all at once, I asked myself and said, "Why is it that those who are not married are earnestly praying to get married, while those who are married are looking for ways to get out? And many of those who are standing seems to be enduring, rather than standing?"

There was a week that almost all those who called me for prayers, it was about marriage breakup. I thought to myself, "What exactly is happening?"

It got to a point I wanted to start thinking if marriage is worth all the troubles. But then, the Holy Spirit softly whispered to my heart and said, *"From the beginning, it was not so."*

God did not plan for marriage to be what we have made it become today. Yes, it is we (human beings) who thwarted God's marriage and family design.

From the scripture above, you get a picture of God's plan for marriage and the family system. God created man and woman and joined them together for life. He said in Genesis 3:24:

> "Therefore a man shall leave his father and his mother, and shall cleave unto his wife: and they shall be one flesh."

If we truly consider this scripture, it's not possible for one to divorce himself or herself. So God never ordained divorce in marriage. Yes, He can heal, open new doors, and give second chances, but it was never His plan in the first place.

It's the devil that is planting all the seeds that destroy the marriage and family system. The reason is that once the devil can disorganize a marriage, home and family, he has succeeded in inflicting so much pain that generations will never forget. Remember that it was devil's attack on the first home that landed humanity in the problem it's facing today.

This is the more reason why we need to embrace the call to regular prayer for our marriages, homes and the family unit.

Here's the thing. If you are not married but hope to do so, you should go ahead and pray these prayers. They'll speak for your future marriage.

If you have a great home at the moment, then target a family or two that is currently going through stress and bring them before God using these prayers and decrees. As you intercede for others, heaven intercedes for you.

> ***God's ultimate desire is for us to have a healthy relationship, one that is filled with peace, prosperity, love and mutual respect.***

If you are currently having a heat in your home, marriage, and relationship, arise and start sending fire against all the anti-marriage demons against your life. Begin to pray for divine help and intervention. Don't stand there and watch the devil destroy your marriage and home.

If there's nothing wrong with or in your marriage, great. But you still need to continuously pray for your marriage and lift up your spouse, children, family, and everyone to God in prayers, every day, and pray for others as well. Don't forget, whatever you make happen for others, God makes happen for you, too.

By regularly praying and speaking God's promises over your home, you'll build a spiritual covering to prevent the enemy from gaining entry in any way and set your family on the path to fulfilling God's plans for your lives.

And please note that this section is not intended to blame anyone regarding any wrong thing happening in the marriage at the moment. It is to stir you to pray for your family, home, and marriage.

God's will for your marriage is abounding peace and prosperity. Don't accept anything short of that. Expect miracles to start happening in your home as you start praying henceforth.

PRAYERS

Part 1: Personal declarations to rekindle faith in your marriage

Read these scriptures and make the attendant declarations out and loud. Let the words enter your spirit, and God's power will be made manifest in your life.

....

1. 1 Peter 4:8 - Above all, love each other deeply, because love covers over a multitude of sins.

Declare: *"Heavenly Father, I declare my love for my partner this day and forever. I declare that I will protect, forgive and overlook my spouse's errors, and dwell on his/her strengths henceforth, in Jesus name."*

---

2. Ecclesiastes 4:12 - Though one may be overpowered, two can defend themselves. A cord of three strands is not quickly broken."

Declare: *I declare that I am united in spirit, soul, and body with my partner. I declare that our love and union cannot be broken by man or demons, in Jesus name.*

---

3. Ephesians 4:2-3 - Be completely humble and gentle; be patient, bearing with one another in love. Make every effort to keep the unity of the spirit through the bond of peace.

Declare: *"I declare this day that I will be enveloped with humility, gentleness, peace, and patience in my relationship,* *even as I will make every effort to make my marriage work and be an example to others, in Jesus name"*

---

4. Psalm 34:3-9: ₃Trust in the Lord and do good; dwell in the land and enjoy safe pasture. ₄ Take delight in the Lord, and he will give you the desires of your heart. Commit your way to the Lord; trust in him, and he will do this:

₆He will make your righteous reward shine like the dawn, your vindication like the noonday sun. Be still before the Lord and wait patiently for him; do not fret when people succeed in their ways when they carry out their wicked schemes.

₈Refrain from anger and turn from wrath; do not fret—it leads only to evil. ₉For those who are evil will be destroyed, but those who hope in the Lord will inherit the land.

Declare: *Because my hope and delight are in the Lord God Almighty, I declare that I inherit peace, love, and prosperity in my marriage. I declare that my home shall be a center for peace, from where the light of salvation shall be extended to all the nations, in Jesus name.*

---

5. **Philippians 2:3-7** – ₃Do nothing out of selfish ambition or vain conceit. Rather, in humility value others above yourselves, ₄not looking to your interests but each of you to the interests of the others. In your relationships with one another, have the same mindset as Christ Jesus: Who, being in very nature God, did not consider equality with God something to be used to his own advantage; instead, he made himself nothing by taking the very nature of a servant, being made in human likeness.

Declare: *"From this day, O LORD, I declare that I have the mind of Christ. I declare that my interests are not to please myself but to please my partner, and together we shall dwell in love and peace that passes all understanding, in Jesus name."*

---

6. **Isaiah 30:21** - And thine ears shall hear a word behind thee, saying, This is the way, walk ye in it, when ye turn to the right hand, and when ye turn to the left.

Declare: *"O LORD, I declare my total dependence on You in my marriage. Cause my ears to hear and my heart to perceive Your instructions over issues that crop up in my marriage and lead me to handle them with utmost sensitivity towards the glory of your name, in Jesus name"*

7. **James 1:5-6** - If any of you lack wisdom, let him ask of God, that giveth to all men liberally, and upbraideth not; and it shall be given him.

Declare: *Heavenly Father, I declare that I lack the wisdom to run my home and have a successful marriage. I declare my total helplessness without Your help. Please give me the wisdom to be a better partner and make my marriage work, in Jesus name"*

Part 2: Rebuke the Devil Over Your Marriage

Put the name of your spouse where necessary

....

Heavenly Father, I thank You for giving us the power to tread upon snakes and scorpions and nothing will harm us. Thank You for giving us power over the devil, and his works through the name of Jesus Christ. (Luke 10:19)

Father, Lord, I bring every sin in my life and in the life of my spouse that is creating a distance between us and you and giving the devil and legal right to attack and afflict our home. I confess these sins, Lord, and plead for Your mercy and forgiveness in Jesus name.

I pray today, O Lord, by Your fire, close every legal ground that satan is using to accuse and attack our marriage in the spirit, in Jesus name.

Now, I decree that satan has no right in my marriage and my home anymore. I command all of the negative links and connections the devil is using against me and my home to be destroyed, in Jesus name.

Today, O LORD, I declare that every work of darkness against my marriage and home is destroyed, in Jesus name

---

It is written that in the name of Jesus Christ every knee must bow (Philippians 2:10). And that whatever we bind here on earth is bound in heaven, and whatever we loose is loosed. I, therefore, command the spirits of strife, anger, misunderstanding, selfishness, greed, hatred and lust of the flesh, to be bound out of my marriage and be cast into the abyss, in Jesus name.

I reject every contrary spirit of lies projected from the kingdom of darkness against my spouse and me and command them to go back into abyss right now. I nullify every form of witchcraft attacks being carried out against my marriage and home, in Jesus name.

O God of justice, arise and judge any man or woman secretly or openly working against our marriage. Lord, they are not working against me, but You, for You are the creator of marriage, not me. Therefore, Lord, arise and bring judgment on all their works, and save my marriage, in Jesus name.

My Father, My Father, I will not accept anything other than your perfect will for my life in my marriage. No strange man or woman will ruin my home. I send back all strange men and women working to destroy my marriage to wherever they are coming from I command them to lose their grips on my spouse and my marriage, in Jesus name

---

Deliverance by Fire

Fire from heaven, rain on all agents of darkness working against my marriage in the spirit and the physical. I command their operations and activities to be destroyed today, in Jesus name.

By the Blood of Jesus Christ, I release my spouse from every witchcraft spells, hexes, curses, and manipulations. I claim my spouse's total deliverance and restoration from the influences of these attacks, in Jesus name.

I proclaim Jesus Christ as the only LORD and Savior of my marriage and home. I declare blessings, prosperity, joy, provision, divine guidance and protection over my home, in Jesus name

---

In the Mighty name of Jesus Christ, I bind the demons of divorce against my marriage. I nullify every generational curse working from my family or my spouse's family to bring divorce in my marriage, in Jesus name.

Every spirit of adultery coming from negative soul ties, family lineage, and bad association, I command you to stop your works forthwith, and I chase you into the abyss today in Jesus name

---

I sanctify my marriage and my spouse in the spirit realm and declare once again that our marriage will be Holy unto the Lord, in Jesus name

---

Father, Lord, I eject from our home every spirit of suspicion, debt, anger, and fighting. I command fire to destroy every altar and stump of the devil in my family in Jesus name.

I plead the Blood of Jesus Christ over my marriage and my spouse. I claim total restoration in our marriage today. I will have peace, love, and prosperity in this marriage, in Jesus name.

O LORD my Father, today, I dethrone every evil throne that has been raised against my marriage and family. I command every force of wickedness working against my spouse or any member of this family for that matter to be destroyed this day, and every power assigned to cause spiritual rebellion and destruction in this home, to perish by fire, in Jesus name.

O Lord, I rededicate my marriage to You and speak Your blessings in our home once again, in Jesus name.

Part 3: Pray for someone you know whose marriage is under attack

Dear Heavenly Father, I come before You this day and present the marriage of ....and ....to You. Lord, there is nothing impossible before You. What is impossible with man is possible with You. And the hearts of every man are in your hand; You can turn them wherever You will.

So, Lord, I ask that You revive this husband and wife, and draw them back to each other in love and happy union. Renew their love and desire for one another once again, in Jesus name.

I pray, Lord, take away the conflicts and strife that exist between them right now and heal the hurts they are going through, in Jesus name.

Father, imbue them with understanding and tenderness of heart for each other once again and take away this strange urge they have against themselves, in Jesus name.

I stand in the authority given to me by You through Jesus Christ, that whatever I bind here on earth is bound in heaven and whatever I loose on earth is loosed in heaven. Today, I bind the demons causing conflicts, strife, division, pain, misunderstanding and confusion between .... and .... I send these demons bound back into the abyss, in Jesus name.

I command fire from heaven to destroy every witchcraft manipulation and influence over their marriage today. May every agent of darkness working to tear them apart be torn apart today and perish by fire, in Jesus name.

I bind the demons of adultery, insecurity, fear, and anger in the marriage of .... and .... in Jesus name. I cast these demons into the abyss and command their marriage set free today, in Jesus name

---

Father, I release Your peace in their marriage and decree total restoration of love and prosperity once again, in their home, in Jesus name.

Amen.

FOR FURTHER READING

Genesis 2

Day 16: Praying Against Dream Robbers

"For God speaks again and again, in dreams, in visions of the night when deep sleep falls on men as they lie on their beds. He opens their ears in times like that and gives them wisdom and instruction, causing them to change their minds, and keeping them from pride, and warning them of the penalties of sin, and keeping them from falling into some trap." – Job 33:14-18 (TLB)

I've heard people boldly say that they do not believe in dreams. That's probably because they've had many funny dreams that they didn't like and understand. They've probably tried to pray to understand more of their dreams but found it hard. So they accepted that dreams are nothing.

Unfortunately, dreams are powerful avenues of communication with the spirit world. Yes, you don't have to be led by all your dreams, but you have to learn to listen through them from time to time if you must have a victorious life. Many times your dreams will give you clear pictures of what to do about your predicament or even tell you about what's coming so that you can pray.

Many people's problems began with their dreams. They probably had dreams that bothered them when they woke up but didn't do much. Their lives may be fine and things going on well, so they thought, *"what kind of useless dream is this?"*

Here's the thing: it's possible that you have meaningless dreams from time to time. But don't use because of that and say that dreams are nothing. According to our text above, God will send you dreams, again and again, to save you from pride, sin, and traps. But what happens if you are the kind of person who says dreams are useless? You'll likely fall into those sins, continue in your pride, and fall into traps.

Pray this prayer now:

Heavenly Father, please forgive me for ignoring my dreams and not paying attention to see if you are the One trying to guide me, and show me what to do, in Jesus name.

You have probably seen too many things in your dreams and ignored many of them. You're probably saying, *"If God wants to give me a dream, He will give me the dreams that I understand."*

Well, go through the scriptures, you'll see that God speaks through parables most times. In many places, He spoke by using animals and images that required interpretations. What would have happened if those persons involved thought that what they saw was useless? Sure, they would continue in their pride, and fall into the traps that satan set for them. And we may probably not even hear of them.

Yes, dreams can come from self (multitude of busyness); they can come from the devil, and they can also come from God. So you shouldn't say because a particular dream seems to be a play of your subconscious mind, that you don't need to listen through your dreams.

Using Your Dreams to Fight Your Battles

A sister had a dream where she was bleeding. Then in a flash, in the same dream, she saw herself with a child and then the child was taken from her. She woke up and couldn't understand it all, so she didn't do much to reject satan's plans. But some months later, she lost her job and began to face many problems in her marriage.

A brother had a dream where he was shot by an unknown person with a gun. After one week or so, his stomach began to swell. It got so bad that he looked like a pregnant woman.

> When you have certain dreams, don't just walk away and do nothing. No one is saying

> you should be afraid. But wait on the Lord and reject the dream if they don't look good, or ask for wisdom on what to do.

Dreams are one of the ways that God speaks to us today (Joel 2:28, Acts 2:17). It is one of the ways we connect with the spirit world to receive instructions for our lives, learn about evil plans, and strategize on how to protect ourselves through prayers and wisdom. Understanding your dreams can help you determine God's direction on something. It can help you understand what's happening with some of the things you're praying about.

> Listening through your dreams can help you re-strategize your prayers over something and gain victory much quicker than just binding and casting every day.

So if you've not been paying enough attention to your dreams, let's pray today to address this situation. If you're always dreaming and not remembering your dreams, let's pray against spiritual dream robbers.

Joseph would have divorced Mary when he found out she was pregnant, but God sent him a dream that convinced him that the pregnancy was of God. He went ahead with the marriage. After Jesus was born, God sent two more dreams, one to tell

Joseph to take his family to Egypt so Herod could not kill Jesus, and another to tell him Herod was dead and that he could return home (Matthew 1:20; 2:13).

If Joseph had decided to fast and pray or go to the mountain to wait on the Lord when he had the dream to escape, he would have been trapped. The dreams were a means of protection from satan's traps.

> When we're asleep, we're away from all kinds of distractions, worries, and thoughts. The type of peace and quietness we have during sleep connects us to the spirit world from where we're able to receive spiritual directions and instructions

From today, Don't shrug off your dreams and say they are a result of excessive food or because of the environment where you are. While those may have some contributions, dreams often speak of something much more different from the pictures, scenes, and activities of the dream.

What to Do With Your Dreams

The first and most important rule about listening through your dreams is this: *If you have a similar dream more than once, or twice, you need to pay serious attention.* You need to begin to ask yourself what's happening and figure out the right response. The Bible says that God speaks once, but we hear it twice or more, and even still do not perceive what He is saying.

Step 1: Write out any part of your dream that you remember, as you are more prone to forget your dreams once you walk away from your bed. Don't bother about the meanings of your dreams immediately you wake up. Pen down any aspect that you could still remember. This way, if this is something God is sending your way, days or months later, when you go through them and others, the dots will connect.

Step 2: Don't depend on outsiders to interpret your dream. While this is not a sin, your dreams are directly for you. If you're going to depend on social media interpretation, you'll be misled. Yes, people can attempt to interpret your dreams, but no one can interpret the exact message God may be sending your way. If you had a dream and I had a similar dream, the meanings will inevitably be different (in some way) to each of us.

Step 3: Pray about the dream. The Bible says in James 1:5, *If any of you lack wisdom, let him ask of God, who gives to all men liberally, and upbraideth not; and it shall be given him.* When you pray, somehow, you'll learn what the LORD is trying to tell you, and you'll know what to do. Some dreams will require that you take action in that direction. Some will require that you spend some time (maybe with some fasting) to pray over the matter. While others will need that you should either forget about it or expect its manifestation.

Step 4: Judge your dream with the Word of God. The Bible says that "the spiritual man judges all things, and does not subject himself to man's judgments" (1 Corinthians 2:15, Emphasis mine). Always compare what the dream is saying with what the Bible has already said. If what the dream is speaking is sending fear – pray. Use scriptures to counter the contents of the dream. If it is speaking faith, breakthrough, success, victory, then claim it.

Step5: Be led by the Holy Spirit. There's a whole world of difference between having a dream and being led by the dream. When you have dreams, turn them over to the LORD and allow the Holy Spirit to give you the right meanings and guide you on what to believe, or do. Don't glorify dreams, or make them a source of worry. Use them to pray and discern the leading of God through His Holy Spirit.

PRAYERS

Please pray these prayers in the midnight

Deliverance by Fire

....

Dear Heavenly Father, give me the wisdom to listen through my dreams and understand when You're speaking to me and what You're speaking to me about.

Let the Blood of Jesus Christ, sanctify my spirit, soul, and mind today.

May every wrong thoughts I've nurtured before now regarding my dreams be wiped away, in Jesus name.

Lord, open my eyes to any sin in my life that will empower demons to succeed in their attacks against me in the dream, in Jesus name.

By the Blood of Jesus Christ, Lord, I renounce all habitual sins in my life that opens the door for evil manipulations and attacks in my dreams, in Jesus name.

Every evil power that works in my mind, causing me to forget or lose my dreams, cease today, in Jesus Christ name.

Every dream polluters projected against me, I send them back to the abyss, in Jesus name.

Every spiritual arrow from the dream, I call you out today, be destroyed in Jesus name.

In the Everlasting name of Jesus Christ, I renounce every affliction, sickness, struggling, financial crisis, marital disappointments, and failure, projected into my life from the dream world, in Jesus name.

O Lord, send fire from heaven to break and shatter every chain, and prison in my life, originating from witchcraft activities in my dreams, in Jesus name.

All you evil robbers that come to attack me in the dream, tormenting me, and making me forget my dreams, run mad today and run into the abyss, in Jesus name.

Deliverance by Fire

Lord, let fire destroy every evil object, incision, instrument, and tool that has attached themselves to my spirit, soul, or body from the dream world, in Jesus name.

I command every battle going on against my life, my health, and my marriage, that started from the dream, seize today, in the name of Jesus Christ.

I crush all powers monitoring my life in the dream today. I command them to perish by fire, in Jesus name.

Lord, I recover by fire all virtues, blessings, and breakthroughs stolen from me in the past in the dream, in the name of Jesus Christ.

I claim total restoration in every aspect of my life – my marriage, family, career, health, spirituality, ministry, business and relationship. Whatever I have lost in life as a result of jokingly or ignorantly ignoring dreams that God sent to me, by the Blood of Jesus Christ, I claim restoration today, in Jesus name.

I pray today, LORD, open thou my spiritual eyes and understanding to hear what You are telling me through my dreams henceforth, in Jesus name.

Amen.

FOR FURTHER READING

Joel 2 and Acts 2

Day 17: The Power of Parental Blessings

Culled from my book, **Prayers that Break Curses**

O yes, we are talking about deliverance. But permit me to tell you a bit about parental blessings. It's something that may be working for or against you.

Yes, your parents' blessings or curses on you can be responsible for the benefits or difficulties you're experiencing now. That is why reviewing your relationship with your parents is a big factor in your pursuit for total deliverance.

Remember, deliverance is an inside job. The devils outside can't withstand us if we deal with the devils inside. So we have to really look at these things as we pray for deliverance and breakthrough.

Have you ever wondered why the first commandment with a promise attached to it has to do with our relationship with our parents? The Book of Ephesians 6:1-3 says, *"Children, obey your parents in the Lord, for this is right. 'Honor your father and mother,' which is the first commandment with promise: 'that it may be well with you and you may live long on the earth.'"*

A parent's love is the strongest and most enduring love that exists in the world, except God's love. In the scriptures, children always craved the blessings of their parents. I've asked myself many times, *"why would these men value ordinary pronouncements from their parents – especially their fathers – so much as to struggle for it?"*

But the answer is simple:

> *Parental pronouncements create potent forces that accompany us all through our lives, working out good or evil. If they are positive pronouncements, they produce good outcomes; and if they are negative pronouncements, they create problems. This is a divine principle.*

You can't change it. I can't change it.

Your parents are not just ordinary fellows. They have God-given powers to influence the outcomes of your life with their words or thoughts.

And yes, your parents here does not just mean your biological parents. They include anyone with parental authority over you – such as your stepdad or mum, adopted parents, and guardians -those who are seeing you through life. You need their blessings.

DON'T PLAY WITH PARENTAL BLESSINGS

Yes, our parents may not always be right, but dishonoring and causing them pain creates problems for us eventually. You can disagree with your parents over certain issues without letting it become a problem. For example, it's your right to decide who to marry, where to worship, where to live, and jobs to take as an adult. Sometimes, some parents want to dictate these things. If what they are saying is not what you want, you can disagree, but it shouldn't turn into crisis.

The Bible says: *Whoever curses his father or his mother, his lamp will be put out in deep darkness* (Proverbs 20:20). The Amplified Bible renders this verse thus: **'Whoever curses his father or his mother, his lamp of life will be extinguished in time of darkness.'** While the Living Bible says: *'God puts out the light of the man who curses his father or mother.'*

Dishonoring your parents, hurting them, or mistreating them, puts you in enmity with God. That is, God will be the one fighting you. You'll fast, pray, have hands laid on you, yet the problem doesn't get solved, because God is the one responsible for what you're going through – as a result of maltreating your parents.

This is one of the biggest mysteries I've seen working against many people, including Christians. You can't treat your parents like they're nothing and expect life to be fair to you. I was praying with a lady some time ago and was inspired to tell her to call her mother and ask for her prayers and blessings. She later said to me, *"When I called my mom and told her I was calling to ask her forgiveness and blessings, she was stunned. After all said and done, she told me I did the right thing, and therefore it would be well with me."*

"But pastor," she continued. *"I never expected that my mom had some unsaid grievances against me. I thought all was well all these years."*

Sometimes we have maltreated our parents, and out of love, they kept it all inside themselves. They never spoke out. Unfortunately, these actions of disrespect trigger spiritual curses to operate.

The Bible says:

> **Cursed is anyone who dishonors their father or mother. Then all the people shall say, "Amen!"** - Deuteronomy 27:16

> **The eye that mocks a father and scorns to obey a mother will be picked out by the ravens of the valley and eaten by the vultures**. - Proverbs 30:17

Deliverance by Fire

If you've disrespected your parents in the past, go back and say sorry. By going back to say sorry and getting their blessings, you'll stop many unknown sufferings in your life.

A man of God I respect so much once shared a story with me. One day he got worried that he was not experiencing results commensurate with his efforts and prayers in the ministry. So he decided to fast and pray and seek divine revelation. While praying, the LORD revealed to him that he had disrespected his father many years ago and needed to get his father's forgiveness and blessing.

That was a surprising revelation because he had been in ministry for close to 20 years. And as far as he could tell, he did not have any grudges with his dad. He thought his dad was okay with him as they were relating well.

Well, he decided to try out the revelation and impression he had. He bought gifts and traveled home to see his old man. As they were discussing, he enquired from him if there was a grievance he was holding against him. He explained to him that children are, many times, filled with childish exuberances. That if there was something he had done while growing up that he still remembers, he should forgive him. Surprisingly, the old man still remembered an incidence of disrespect and letdown he had caused him while growing up as a young man. He hadn't forgotten that event, even though it was many years ago. They discussed it, and he prayed for him.

He spent some time with his dad and then returned to his ministry base. Two weeks later, someone gave him a car gift. A month or so later, another person gave him a plot of land. He started getting so blessed that he wondered why he didn't discover this and do it earlier.

You see, the truth is that our parents may not have been so kind to us. But they are still the source we came into this world. We must do the best we can to honor them and get their blessings. The simple act of getting our parent's blessings has the power to neutralize many years of hardship.

I know there are exceptions, like when we have been maltreated by our parents. However, even in such situations, we must not ascribe judgment and vengeance to ourselves. We must forgive, pray for them, and seek their blessings, not because we have not been hurt, but because we must move forward. The person who forgives actually does himself a greater good.

HONOR YOUR PARENTS

How do you *"Honor your father and your mother, as the Lord your God has commanded you, so that you may live long and that it may go well with you in the land the Lord your God is giving you?"*

There are specific ways to honor your parents.

- By praying for them
- By caring for their needs, especially as they grow in age
- By respecting them
- By appreciating them in words and actions
- By celebrating them always
- By enduring and forgiving their mistakes and errors
- By listening to their counsels and valuing their opinions even if you're not going to follow them.

Parental blessings are a great asset you need in life.

BLESS YOUR CHILDREN NO MATTER WHAT

There's an adage in my tribe that says, *"It is the elder's heart that lets go for peace to reign."* Holding grudges against your children is not good. Yes, we know, children can be insensitive. But our hearts must forgive and bless no matter what.

We, also, as parents, must always remember that the words we speak to and over our children have strong powers to create their realities eventually. So even when we are trying to discipline our children, let us watch the words we release on them. The Bible also counsels us not to aggravate our children willfully, and so lead them towards rebellion. There's got to be a balance as Colossians 3:20-21 says:

20 Children, obey your parents in everything. This pleases the Lord. 21 Fathers, don't upset your children. If you are too hard to please, they might want to stop trying (ERV).

PRAYERS

Almighty Father, the maker of heaven and earth, creator of family and the home system, I come to You today with thanks. I appreciate Your wisdom in establishing the family system, through which Your purpose on earth is fulfilled. Be praised forever and ever, in Jesus name.

Today, O Lord, I thank You for my parents and guardians. I thank You for giving them the grace to bring me to this world. I thank You for enabling them to care for and protect my siblings and me over the years. Receive all the praise in Jesus name.

Deliverance by Fire

Dear Lord, I ask for forgiveness, in any way I have dishonored and disrespected my parents or guardians in the past. Father, I was ignorant. Please have mercy on me. You said in Psalm 30:5 says that Your anger is but for a moment, Your favor is for life; weeping may endure for a night, but joy comes in the morning.

Father, in Your mercy and favor, remember me, in Jesus name.

Lord, I pray today that You heal and restore my relationship with my parents and guardians. Give me the grace to forgive them, in any way I feel they haven't treated me right in the past.

As I take new steps to make amends with them, O Lord, may Your power prevail in our hearts, and may Your peace, love, and fear be established in our emotions once more, in Jesus name.

From this day, O Lord, I bring before the Blood of Jesus Christ every curse, negative words, and evil pronouncements from my parents, guardians, and teachers in the past. I receive deliverance from the consequences of these statements from today, in Jesus name.

Every spiritual door opened in my life, health, and family as a result of past pronouncements from my parents, guardians and teachers, O Lord, I close them today, in Jesus name.

And I decree healing and restoration from every hurt and pain affecting our lives as a result of these past pronouncements, in Jesus name

---

Dear Holy Spirit, please uproot and flush out every seed of bitterness, malice and fighting in me and my parents. Let these evil seeds creating a distance between us be flushed away today, in Jesus name.

As a parent also, Lord, I pray that all curses, grudges, negative pronouncements and evil wishes, I have uttered or wished in the past, against my children and those under my care, be nullified today, in Jesus name.

Today, I exercise myself onto forgiveness and willfully forgive my children, grandchildren, and anyone whom I cared for in the past that offended me. I drop all resentments and weights against every one of them, and release them all from whatever curse happening in their lives as a result of this harbored pain in my heart, in Jesus name.

I speak blessings and peace in the name of the Lord on my children, stepchildren, grandchildren, and everyone connected to me. I decree that it shall be well with all of them.

I proclaim my offspring blessed. I declare my generation blessed. I declare my family members blessed. I pronounce my home healed and blessed, in Jesus name. Amen

FOR FURTHER READING

Exodus 20, Deuteronomy 28

Day 18: Deliverance of the Tongue

Culled from my book, **Prayers That Break Curses**

Say to them, 'As I live,' says the Lord, 'just as you have spoken in My hearing, so I will do to you

- Numbers 14:28

It sounds strange to talk about the deliverance of the tongue, right? Well, I needed to remind you that your words to yourself every day, about your life, career, future, and home are working for or against you in many ways.

I could pray for you, lay hands on you, and fast for forty days on your behalf, but if your words are consistently filled with negativity, fear, and complaints, nothing will happen. Your words will either enable your prayers or invalidate them, because you have divine authority over your life.

Fifteen years or so ago, we had this friend of ours who was very prayerful. We always envied his prayer life. He would wake up in the midnight and pray for four hours or more at a stretch. Usually, when you wake up to pray, he's praying.

When you're done praying, he's still praying. No one could match his prayer life.

Unfortunately, ask him about life, and you'll hear the worse negative arguments from him. When he speaks, he speaks of discouragement, fear, failure, and how life has messed him up. I usually wonder how he's able to spend hours praying and never sees anything positive about life. Try to encourage him, and he'll tell you to forget about it. It was a paradox too profound for me to comprehend.

Yes, he had experienced a lot of challenges before discerning the call of God for his life. Sadly, these setbacks had eaten too deep into him that irrespective of his powerful prayer life, he didn't expect much from life, and he was always quick to admit it in conversations. Guess what: a few years ago, that's like thirteen years after, when I bumped into him, his experiences had not changed much from the things he was always saying those years. And the worse was that he was still filled with such damming negativity about life.

The truth is that life is not easy; we all experience challenges and setbacks day in day out. But the best we can do to ourselves is being positive. We must not allow our problems to define our words and expectations for the future. If we do, these words become self-imposed arrows against us, working and creating more limitations that we'll always wonder where our problems are coming from.

If you regularly speak faith-filled words no matter the circumstances you're facing, you'll create energies that will eventually lead to blessings and positive experiences. But if you continuously speak fear and complaint-filled words, you develop more problems as returns.

The book of Proverbs 18:21 says: *"Death and life are in the power of the tongue, and those who love it will eat its fruit."*

Jesus said, *"For by your words you will be justified, and by your words, you will be condemned"* (Matthew 12:37).

If I ask you and say, *'how's life?'* And you say…

- *'Men, it's not easy.'*

- *'Things are so hard now.'*

- *'I've tried all I could, but there is no way.'*

- *'I'm just parching and managing.'*

- *'I'm dying.'*

- *'There is no hope.'*

- *'These children will kill me.'*

- *'This job is killing me.'*

- *'I'm just wasting away here.'*

- *'My husband is just a big pain.'*

- *'My wife is troublesome. She is killing me.'*

- *'This economy is biting so hard.'*

- *'I just keep getting frustrated and frustrated.'*

- *'I'll be dead soon.'*

- *'God hates me. He doesn't answer my prayers'*

- *'This child is just so hopeless.'*

Using words like these may seem like you're just stating how things are at the moment, but those are strong negative affirmations that eventually create those realities. The Bible says:

....

Proverbs 13:3 - *He who guards his mouth preserves his life, but he who opens wide his lips shall have destruction.*

Proverbs 16:24 - *Pleasant words are like a honeycomb, sweetness to the soul and health to the bones.*

Proverbs 21:23 - *Whoever guards his mouth and tongue keeps his soul from troubles.*

Matthew 15:18 - *But those things which proceed out of the mouth come from the heart, and they defile a man.*

Ephesians 4:29 - *Let no corrupt word proceed out of your mouth, but what is good for necessary edification, that it may impart grace to the hearers.*

....

The scriptures are not joking with these warnings. Your words are either making or unmaking you. That is why deliverance is not complete without talking about the power resident in your tongue for your good or otherwise.

PRAYERS

Heavenly Father, You said that the power of death and life is in the tongue; and that we will be justified or condemned by our words (Prov. 18:21, & Matt. 12:37). Lord, I know that Your Words are ever true. Heaven and earth will pass away but Your Words will not.

Lord, I acknowledge that I have used my words in ways that were not decent and pleasing to You. I have used my words to hurt others, speak negative things about my life, partner, children, family, and my nation. Father, I now ask You to forgive all my wrong use of words from past to present, in Jesus name.

Precious Blood of Jesus Christ, sanctify my tongue and purify my heart. Empower me to be a carrier and speaker of life, health, encouragement, and peace from today onwards, in Jesus name.

Whatever pain and hurt I have brought upon myself, my family, my career, my children, and my family, as a result of my wrong use of words in the past, Heavenly father, heal and restore me today, in Jesus name

---

In the name of Jesus Christ, I decree that no corrupt word will proceed out of my mouth henceforth, but what is good for edification, imparting grace to the hearers, health to the sick, and blessings to all, in Jesus name.

Today, I willingly command myself to put away all forms of bitterness, wrath, anger, clamor, malice, and evil speaking *from my mouth. I command myself to be kind to others, tenderhearted, forgiving, and ever ready to be a blessing, in the name of Jesus Christ.*

I break any curse I have imposed on myself ignorantly, through my use of negative words, complaints, anger, fear, and anxiety, in Jesus name.

It is written that the days of ignorance, the Lord overlooks (Acts 17:30). Therefore, if there are any evil happening in my life and family as a result of my negative confessions in the past, I command them to stop today.

I replace all self-inflicted pains and events in my life today with God's favor, peace and breakthrough, in Jesus name.

I bless myself from now onwards; I bless my home; I bless my career; I bless my family; I bless my church, and I bless my children.

Henceforth, my going out shall be a blessing and my coming back shall be a blessing. I shall be blessed in the city; I shall be blessed in the country.

When and where others are saying there is a casting down, I shall be saying there is a lifting up, in Jesus name.

O LORD, according to your Word in Romans 8:28, everything is working out for my good. I am a blessing to my family. I am a blessing to my country. I am a blessing to my generation. In the name of Jesus.

Amen.

FOR FURTHER READING

Matthew 12

Day 19: Breaking the Curse of Debt

"Let's do a test," I said, looking at the congregation. "Is there anyone here who likes to be in debt?"

No one said yes.

"Okay," I continued. "Is there anyone here who is currently in some sort of debt and seriously wants to be free?"

Almost every hand went up. Okay, let's say about seventy percent of the audience.

One crucial area of life that believers are stumbling today is on the area of debt. I see it as a curse because it is holding a lot of people down from freely pursuing God's plans for their lives.

Many times, debt is a consequence of our actions and poor business and financial decisions. Sometimes, too, it can be a result of forces outside our control. Whatever is responsible for your debts, God wants you to do something about it and be free from them.

I know that the issue of debt is a serious one because we receive requests for prayers every day for debt cancellation and miracles for urgent financial needs. As I think about the situation more and more every day, and pray, I realize that believers need to sit down and learn God's word on debt. While I've received testimonies of miraculous debt cancellations, many others haven't had the same miracles happen for them. Of course, God is not partial. He is good to every one of us. But I've learned that prayers are not enough when dealing with the issue of debt.

So before we pray, let's look at a few scriptures on debt. Remember, God's word is the key to healing and deliverance. For *"He sent his word, and healed them, and delivered them from their destructions"* (Psalm 107:20)

God can work miracles on your debt, but it will be quicker when you know what He's saying about debt so that you're able to prevent subsequent debt trap.

WHY YOU'RE IN DEBT

Let's start by saying that you're not in debt because you're not rich. Think about it. Those who are rich are also in debt. The truth is that if you had more money, you're likely to still be in debt.

> *Yes, you can be broke and not be in debt; and you can have money and still be in debt.*

So you're in debt because the financial system of this world is configured to keep you in debt. It's one way satan gets to keep people in perpetual worry trap. And we bought *debt benefits* wholly because it satisfies our immediate pleasure. However, you're going to choose whether to surrender to this worldly system or the heavenly system.

Worldly system says: debt is a tool. If you're in debt, borrow more money.

Finance books say: you need leverage. Learn to use Other People's Money (OPM) to get what you want.

The banks say: we'll give you a loan. You don't need to use your money. Just sign here. Take our credit cards; you can use them any time; we'll wait when you have money so can we take what you owe us.

The real estate companies say: don't miss this property. Don't worry; pay us slowly and progressively, when you can.

Then we read the news and hear that even our governments owe billions and billions of dollars. So somehow, we're sold that it's kinda cool to borrow, borrow, and borrow some more. Our mind tells us, *"If we can have the good lifestyle now and pay later, why not."* Unfortunately, that isn't the whole truth.

You're in debt because your mind tells you that it's not easy to live without debt. Somehow, you grew with this mindset, you read books that encouraged it, and met a financial system that sells it every minute. So life is replaying the results of this distortion on you. To get out of debt, you have to start by reprogramming your mind. You have to start by convincing yourself that you can live without debt and borrowing; that you would better be a lender than a debtor.

> I've been in huge debts before, accidentally incurred, as a result of failed business and unwise agreements. I can tell you that the pressure and stress that debts invite upon us is not what God wants us to live with.

It's understandable that there are situations when borrowing is completely unavoidable, like in medical emergencies, job layoffs, and others. But the whole truth is that borrowing and debt are inviting tomorrow's evil today. We can choose to obey God and let each day carry its burden or continue to invite the burdens of the next day and the coming years on the present.

GOD'S WORD ON DEBT

Let's start the fight on debts by looking at few scriptures and what they are saying to us regarding debts.

1. The debtor is a slave to the creditor: Debt invokes a slavery status on the debtor to the creditor (Proverbs 22:7). This isn't the position Christ wants us to be. He has paid all our debts and made us free. Forcing ourselves in debt is questioning His very work of redemption for us.

2. God wants us to lend to others instead: Sounds like a paradox, right? First, we say a borrower is a slave to the lender. Next, we say, God wants us to lend to others. *"For the Lord, your God will bless you just as He promised you; you shall lend to many nations, but you shall not borrow; you shall reign over many nations, but they shall not reign over you"* (Deuteronomy 15:6, 28:12, Matthew 5:42).

The message is that if there's going to be anyone who will be a slave, then it shouldn't be the people in covenant with God. By being the lenders, we demonstrate that God is enough for us and does supply our needs. This way, we can attract the unbelievers to our God.

3. It is wickedness not to repay debts: - Psalm 37:21 says, *"The wicked borrows and does not repay, but the righteous shows mercy and gives."* And Romans 13:7 (MSG) reads: *"Fulfill your obligations as a citizen. Pay your taxes, pay your bills, and respect your leaders."*

Even though our legal system allows individuals and businesses in suffering to recuperate themselves under the protection of bankruptcy laws, as believers, we have a moral obligation to repay our creditors to the best of our ability.

Applying the bankruptcy laws should only be in very critical situations. This is also the same as praying for debt cancellation. You need to make efforts to repay your debts. You need to pray for a divine provision that will enable you to pay up what you owe. Only resort to praying for debt cancellation when the situation is very critical.

4. Don't be in haste to sign a guarantee for someone: *"Be sure you know a person well before you vouch for his credit! Better refuse than suffer later. Unless you have the extra cash on hand, don't countersign a note. Why risk everything you own? They'll even take your bed!"* (Proverbs 11:15, 22:26-27 - TLB).

There's nothing to add there.

5. Be faithful in the little money you have: *He who is faithful in what is least is faithful also in much, and he who is unjust in what is least is unjust also in much. Therefore if you have not been faithful in the unrighteous mammon, who will commit to your trust the true riches?* (Luke 16:10-11)

6. Don't spend all your money on shopping: *The wise man saves for the future, but the foolish man spends whatever he gets* (Proverbs 21:20 - TLB).

7. Forgive debts owed you: if someone owing you money is unable to repay, and in all honesty, you can see that he is unable, the Bible says to forgive. Exercising forgiveness in such circumstances does not make you a fool. Instead by extending mercy, you obtain mercy in your matters as well (See Matthew 18:21-35 TLB).

8. Be content with what you have: *Stay away from the love of money; be satisfied with what you have. For God has said, 'I will never, never fail you nor* forsake you' (Hebrews 13:5).

....

As you can see, while the Bible did not say that borrowing or debt is a sin, it does make it clear that it is not God's best for us. In fact, the story of the widow in 2Kings 4:1-8 is clear proof that debt can bring severe consequences for family and children. That is why the Apostle Paul counsels us in Romans 13:8 to *"owe no one anything except to love one another, for he who loves another has fulfilled the law."*

HOW TO BE FREE FROM DEBT

Let's face it. There are times that the debts we find ourselves in are not of our own making. They could have been incurred as a result of things that were considered very urgent and essential, or emergency situations. However, there are other times that our debts are a result of our choices and mistakes.

Whichever the case is, we can trust God completely for help and deliverance.

In the Scriptures, our sins are often treated as debts. When we genuinely repent and confess them to God, He forgives us and the process of complete restoration starts. The same can be done with our debts.

Step 1: Pray.

List out all your debts in a paper and take them to the Lord in prayer. Take responsibility and ask for His mercy and forgiveness. Ask God for help with any habit or attitude that led you to those debts. Plead the Blood of Jesus Christ, and ask God for help with the debts.

Debt is a yoke and a weight that tries to keep us down. And God can give us rest from our yokes as we come to Him in faith through Christ Jesus (Matthew 11:28-29)

Sometimes God's help with your debts may not necessarily be about canceling the debts, but about opening doors of new jobs for you so that you can earn more money to be able to pay your debts. Be open while you're praying and tell God you want a way out of those debts. Don't insist He must cancel the indebtedness because He already says you should pay back your debts.

While praying, commit yourself to stay with God's words on money and not the worldly financial system. God wants us to be the lenders and not the debtors. So stop borrowing. Stop going into more debts.

Step 2: Review and begin to deal with habits that lead to debts.

Review your belief about debts and personal actions that keep you in debt. It starts with your mindset. We have a rule in our home, which I learned from my father in the Lord. The rule says: *If we can't afford it, then it's not yet the right time for it.*

Learn to start trusting God for your provisions and not your abilities. Often, we go into debts when we want things and lifestyles that we can't afford at the moment. We may believe that we desperately need those things and then go into debt. But the truth is that if we looked deeper, we didn't need them. There were alternatives (God's ways of escape) that we ignored.

Step 3: Don't run away from your debts

Don't try to cover the shame that the Lord has not covered. It will come back. When our forex and investment business failed, and we ran into huge debts, our creditors dragged us to many different places. It wasn't easy. But thankfully, we never missed a meeting with them. Of course, there were all kinds of threats here and there. But we gently and prayerfully followed through with everything. When many of them saw that we didn't defraud them, they started to calm down and began to pray for us.

Yes, you can be praying for debt cancellation and pleading for God's intervention, but while you're doing that, don't try to act fraudulently by avoiding your creditors. Face your mess with confidence that God will make a way somehow.

Step 4: Recognize God's escape plans.

The Bible says in 1 Corinthians 10:13 that *"No temptation has overtaken you except such as is common to man; but God is faithful, who will not allow you to be tempted beyond what you are able, but with the temptation will also make the way of escape, that you may be able to bear it."*

As you pray and seek God for help and deliverance from debt, He will make a way of escape. First, He will give you the grace to bear the pressures, and sustain your health. Next, he will begin to open new doors for you: New business opportunities, new job offers, and new ideas.

Don't get stuck with expecting miraculous debt cancellations or expecting that your creditors will forget that you owe them money that you fail to recognize and take advantage of God's escape plans. And as soon as you begin to see these new blessings, don't forget your debts.

Step 5: Employ the serpent skill.

Jesus told us to be wise as a serpent but harmless as a dove. One area that the serpent is so good is in the area of negotiation. He negotiated Adam and Even out of the Garden of Eden, and even tried it with Christ, but failed.

As a further step to deal with your debt, negotiate with your creditors. Give them a call. Ask for a soft landing. Let them know you're doing your best. Demand forgiveness of some or all parts of the debt. Many will oblige when they see you honestly want to do something about the debt.

Step 6: Learn about money and investment God's way.

All the suggestions I've outlined above are based on my experience and revelation. They should not replace professional financial counseling. Read books on money and investment God's way, and learn Bible ways to approach finance. One thing I'm sure about is that as you honestly pray and take divinely inspired steps towards your debts, God will make way for you.

PRAYERS

1. Thank God for the Blood of Jesus Christ that cleanses us from all unrighteousness, forgives our debts, and makes us appear before God holy.

2. *Ask God to forgive you for doing things that put you in debt. Tell God you're sincerely sorry for not trusting Him on money in your trying times.*

3. Tell God that you're ready to be a lender and not a borrower anymore. Ask for His power and grace to lend and not to borrow from this day forward.

4. Ask God to deliver you from the slavery of debt, in Jesus name.

5. Pray for courage to trust God more in money matters going forward, and to exercise faith for His provisions always, in Jesus name.

6. Ask God to give you the wisdom to be faithful in small things even as you expect Him to bless you with big things.

7. **Pray:** *Every negative attachment I have with the god of mammon that is speaking against my finances, be destroyed, in Jesus name.*

8. Ask God to show you attitudes and habits that are always putting you in debt and ask for His grace to overcome these habits.

9. Ask God to give you grace and favor with your creditors, so that they will show mercy as you discuss and plan on your debt. Ask God to touch their hearts to work for your favor.

10. **Pray:** *O Lord, help me to recognize and take advantage of the ways of escape that you have provided for me over my debts, in Jesus name.*

11. Ask God to give you new business ideas, opportunities, and jobs that will give help you earn more money to pay your debts.

12. **Pray:** *O Lord, speak on my behalf whenever I talk to my creditors, in Jesus name.*

13. *I bind every spirit of debt and borrowing, and cast them out of my life and family, into the abyss, in Jesus name.*

14. *Blood of Jesus Christ, erase every curse debt, hard labor, and sweating to eat, in Jesus name.*

15. *Holy Ghost fire, consume to ashes every power, every activity, every arrow, in heaven and on earth, that is preventing me from my breakthroughs, in Jesus name.*

16. *By the blood of Jesus Christ, I break every cycle of financial instability in my life, in Jesus name.*

17. *I cancel every debt present in my life right now by the Blood of Jesus Christ, in Jesus name.*

18. *By the Blood of Jesus Christ, I nullify all debts and burdens passed on to me from past generations of my family, spiritually working against my breakthrough, in the name of Jesus Christ.*

19. *I decree that I am free from debt; I decree that I will fulfill the purposes of God for my life; I decree that God is providing all my needs according to His riches in Christ Jesus, in Jesus name.*

20. *Father, Lord, I thank You for giving me wisdom and victory over debts, in Jesus name.*

Amen.

FOR FURTHER READING

2 Kings 4

Day 20: A Prayer of Agreement Against Specific Oppressions

If you're here, then it's likely you've faithfully followed through all the teachings and prayers before this page. It's likely that you earnestly desire God's move in your life and family. It's likely that you sincerely want a new level.

As I write these words, the Holy Spirit would want me to assure you that you got it. *God shall deliver you from all your troubles; yes, He will make His face to shine on you. Henceforth, no evil shall touch you. In famine, He shall redeem you from death, and in war from the power of the sword. He will give you peace.*

Yes, we may not be able to cover every area of life that we need deliverance in this one book. As I look at the prayer requests before me, I see that clearly. So today, I'll be asking you to specifically pray over those specific oppressions in your life or family right now.

This is what we'll do: we'll be praying in agreement and invoking the power of Matthew 18:18-20. It says:

₁₈Assuredly, I say to you, whatever you bind on earth will be bound in heaven, and whatever you loose on earth will be loosed in heaven.

₁₉Again, I say to you that if two of you agree on earth concerning anything that they ask, it will be done for them by My Father in heaven.

₂₀For where two or three are gathered together in My name, I am there in the midst of them."

Jesus means business here. These words may look too simple, but they are what they are. When two or three people pray in agreement, heaven will intervene.

Do you believe that scripture?

Let me tell you something I call prayer bullet. According to me, when you read a scripture, and meditate on it and turn it into prayer, it becomes a prayer bullet sent on a specific errand in the spirit to deal with the issue it was sent for.

As you read those words of Christ, I want you to get it done today. Get someone to come to an agreement with you, to pass a decree regarding the specific oppression going on in your life.

Are there certain oppressions, pains, sufferings, and situations that must dissolve from your life as soon as possible? Take a piece of paper and begin to list them all out right now. When you're done, look them over and say, *"You're all coming to an end."*

Now get someone to pray in agreement with you. You two or three will be passing a decree over those situations. That's what I want to charge you to do on this 20th day of this **Deliverance by Fire** prayer retreat.

Okay, while you're still working on that, come to an agreement with me and pray the prayers below.

PRAYERS

Heavenly Father, I believe in Your Words. They are Yea, and they are, Amen.

Lord, I believe that when I decree a thing, it shall be so. I believe that when I come to an agreement with someone over an issue, it will be done.

O Lord, I come before You today and agree with Brother Daniel Okpara in prayer over these situations listed on this paper. I invoke the power of agreement as stated in Your Word.

O Lord, concerning the following situations:

Deliverance by Fire

....

....

I claim total deliverance at this moment from each one of them, in Jesus name. I command the stones stopping these situations from going away, to be gone this moment, and rolled into the abyss.

I command all the demons responsible for these problems and attacks in my life and family to seize operation forthwith and bound back into the abyss, in Jesus name.

Lord, I decree that I am free from:

....

....

For Jesus came to set me free; I am therefore free indeed, in the Mighty name of Jesus Christ.

Amen.

FOR FURTHER READING

Matthew 18 and Mark 11

Day 21: The Power of Praise in Deliverance

*"Who is like unto thee, O Lord, among the gods? Who is like thee, glorious in holiness, **fearful in praises**, doing wonders?* – Exodus 15:11

God is fearful in praises. He does wonders in praises.

David had endless triumphs and never lost a single battle even though he found himself in devastating situations. The secret was that he had a very close relationship with God and knew how to praise Him.

Through praise, you handover your battles to God because He inhabits in the praises of His people (Psalm 22:3).

Let the high praises of God be in their mouth, and a two-edged sword in their hand; to execute vengeance upon the heathen, and punishments upon the people;
To bind their kings with chains, and their nobles with fetters of iron; to execute upon them the judgment written: this honor have all his saints. Praise ye the Lord. - Psalm 149:6-9

High praise, power praise, heartfelt appreciation will put a two-edged sword in your hand to execute vengeance upon the heathen. Every child of God has this honor. It's time to use it.

Deliverance by Fire

Look at this:

And when he had consulted with the people, he appointed singers unto the Lord, and that should praise the beauty of holiness, as they went out before the army, and to say, Praise the Lord; for his mercy endures forever.

And when they began to sing and to praise, the Lord set ambushments against the children of Ammon, Moab, and mount Seir, which were come against Judah; and they were smitten.

For the children of Ammon and Moab stood up against the inhabitants of mount Seir, utterly to slay and destroy them: and when they had made an end of the inhabitants of Seir, every one helped to kill another. - 2 Chron 20:21-23

Each time I read this story, something tickles in my spirit. How would Jehoshaphat, the king of small Judah, fight the army of three countries allied against him?

Jehoshaphat was instructed to go to this battle with instruments and songs.

Now, how do you explain that to modern army generals? I mean, there you have three nations coming in combat against you, well equipped. And instead of you either calling to negotiate a soft landing, or reaching out to other countries to form your allies, you go to the battle without bows, arrows, and guns, but with instruments singing praises and shouting Hallelujah?

That's the highest level of craziness! But you see, God uses the unwise things of this world to confound the wise.

So beloved, engage the foolishness and craziness of praise today. Declare this 21st day of your prayer retreat a day of radical praise to God. Come before with thanksgiving. Sing and dance before Him, play music and let your heart sing to His Holy name.

> Don't worry about remaining issues and prayer point. Praise God today.

When the army of Jehoshaphat *"began to sing and to praise, the Lord set ambushments against the children of Ammon, Moab, and mount Seir, which were come against Judah; and they were smitten. For the children of Ammon and Moab stood up against the inhabitants of mount Seir, utterly to slay and destroy them: and when they had made an end of the inhabitants of Seir, every one helped to destroy another."*

Your enemies will join themselves to slaughter themselves, in Jesus name.

"Brother Dan," you say, *"are you sure this fasting and prayer declarations really did anything? I don't have any feelings of supernatural yo-yo. Am I alright?"*

Yes, you're absolutely fine. Don't measure your prayers and God's power at work in your life by how you feel. Even when you feel bad and lost, God heard your prayers and is doing great things in your life and family.

It's time to move on to praise.

> **When you praise God, you build Him a habitation. When you praise God, you make Him a sanctuary and activate His dominion. When He is present in His power, the sea disappears; the mountains skip like rams and the little hills like lambs.**

When God appears, darkness disappears. When He is present, the earth will tremble.

David was an addicted praiser. God took him from following the sheep to becoming the king of Israel.

After today, declare a season of praise to God. Spend the next month praising and dancing before Him every night. Your earth will undoubtedly yield her increase.

Let the people praise thee, O God; let all the people praise thee. Then shall the earth yield her increase; and God, even our own God, shall bless us - Psalm 67:5-6

The earth in this passage symbolizes your womb, your mind, your business, your potentials, your family, your career, your children and everything that concerns you. It's time to unleash the power of God for productivity in all areas of your life with the power of praise.

PRAYERS

1. O LORD, I thank You for all You have done in my life, in my home, in the Church and in the nation (1 Chron.16:8--9). Receive my praise and honor in Jesus name.

2. Thank You for Your provisions for my family and me. You have not allowed us to suffer hunger; for this, I say thank You LORD (Deut.8:10, Psalm 34:10).

3. Thank you for our salvation and our heavenly inheritance in Christ Jesus (Col.1:12).

4. Thank You for making us seated with Christ in the heavenly places, far above principalities and powers (Ephesians 2:6).

5. Thank You for our authority over Satan (Luke 10:19).

6. Thank you, Lord, for forgiving us of our sins and healing our diseases (Psalm.103:3).

7. Thank you, Lord, for good health enjoyed throughout the past years and the one we will continue to enjoy (3John 1:2, Exo.15:26).

8. Thank you, Lord, for delivering us from all forms of destruction (Ps.103:4).

9. Thank you, Lord, for satisfying us with all good things (Ps.103:5).

10. Thank you, Lord, for not allowing us to be victims to our enemies (Ps.124:6).

11. Thank you, Lord, for enabling us to escape all the traps the enemy set for us (Ps. 124:7).

12. Thank you, Lord, for fighting all our battles for us so far (Ex.14:14)

13. Thank You, LORD, for the great things You are doing in our lives and family.

14. Father, I know that You are at work in my life. I know that Your light is shining and will forever shine in my ways. For this I say, thank You, LORD, in Jesus name. Amen.

FOR FURTHER READING

Psalm 100, 139, 145

ENDING PRAYER

"Heavenly Father, Mighty Man of war,

The Elshadai

The King of kings, LORD of lords

The Ancient of days

The unmistakable Director

The Father of the fatherless

The Husband of the widow

The Only true God

Jehovah Ropheka

Jehovah Mekadiskenu

Jehovah Shalom

O LORD, I come to Thee this day with praise and dance.

I join the hosts of heaven to praise and magnify Thy Name.

Forever and ever, You remaineth the same

I command my spirit to praise the LORD with all we've got.

For the LORD is good and greatly to be praised.

His mercy endures forever

Addendum: How to Maintain Your Deliverance

After Deliverance, What Next?

"When the unclean spirit has gone out of a person, it passes through waterless places seeking rest, but finds none.

Then it says, 'I will return to my house from which I came.' And when it comes, it finds the house empty, swept, and put in order.

Then it goes and brings with it seven other spirits more evil than itself, and they enter and dwell there, and the last state of that person is worse than the first. So also will it be with this evil generation." – **Matt. 12:43-45**

I write this page in almost all our deliverance and prayer books, because God does not want us to stop at deliverance. He wants us to live in total victory – every day.

In the text above, Jesus is saying that there is a probability that one gets healed or delivered from something and the problem comes back, and the situation even becomes worse. Not because the person wasn't delivered in the first instance, but because the person did not care to maintain their deliverance.

But it doesn't have to be so.

Beyond getting delivered, God wants us to live free from all oppressions; He wants us to be strong and sound. The following Biblical instructions will help you to walk in victory, no matter what the enemies throw at you:

1. PRACTICE ADVANCE FORGIVENESS

Advance forgiveness is forgiving an offense even before it is committed against you. You decide not to harbor hurts and bitterness no matter what. This is because as long as we're on earth, offenses will always come. As we're trying to let one issue go, something happens, and if we're not careful, we'll find ourselves, back and forth, always struggling with hurts from time to time.

Sit down today and tell yourself, *"LORD, help me to forgive offenses and issues even before they happen, in Jesus name."*

Life is too precious to live one moment is someone else's cage.

2. ALLOW NO VACUUM IN YOUR MIND

You've heard that "Nature abhors a vacuum." That's right.

If you allow a vacuum in your mind, something will fill it. If you don't fill your mind with positive things, negative things will automatically load it. There can be no vacuum.

The Bible says: *"Keep this Book of the Law always on your lips; meditate on it day and night, so that you may be careful to do everything written in it. Then you will be prosperous and successful. -* **Joshua 1:8"**

Read the Bible daily, hear faith-filled tapes, and fill your mind with news and stuff that edifies you.

3. GET BUSY FOR GOD

A free life is God's covenant to those who serve Him. You don't have to be a pastor to serve God. There are many service related things you can do to keep yourself connected to God's covenant. Join in sharing tracts, pray genuinely for others, become a volunteer in some community service, go pray for the sick from time to time, reach out to the poor, and so on. Just get busy for the LORD, and no enemy will have grounds over your life

4. LEARN TO EXERCISE YOUR AUTHORITY AND FAITH

It is possible that you experience some form challenges from time to time. Now, this doesn't mean you're no longer free from what you prayed against or that God did not deliver you as you prayed earlier. When you encounter these temporary situations, continually declare the Word of God over your health, even if you take medicines.

Now faith is the assurance (title deed, confirmation) of things hoped for (divinely guaranteed), and the evidence of things not seen [the conviction of their reality—faith comprehends as fact what cannot be experienced by the physical senses]. 2 For by this [kind of] faith the [a]men of old gained [divine] approval - **Hebrews 11:1(AMP).**

6. USE YOUR WORDS RIGHT

Proverbs 18:21 - Death and life are in the power of the tongue: and they that love it shall eat the fruit thereof.

1 Peter 3:10 - For he that will love life, and see good days, let him refrain his tongue from evil, and his lips that they speak no guile

Ephesians 4:29 - Let no corrupt communication proceed out of your mouth, but that which is suitable to the use of edifying, that it may minister grace unto the hearers.

Daniel C. Okpara

GOD

BLESS

YOU

Get in Touch

We love testimonies.

We love to hear what God is doing around the world as people draw close to Him in prayer. If this book has blessed...

Please share your story with us.

Also, please consider giving this book a review on Amazon and checking out our other titles at:

amazon.com/author/danielokpara

Kindly do check out our website at www.BetterLifeWorld.org, and send us your prayer request. As we join faith with you, God's power will be made manifest in your life.

Other Books by the Same Author

1. Prayer Retreat: 21 Days Devotional With Over 500 Prayers & Declarations to Destroy Stubborn Demonic Problems.

2. HEALING PRAYERS & CONFESSIONS

3. 200 Violent Prayers for Deliverance, Healing, and Financial Breakthrough.

4. Hearing God's Voice in Painful Moments

5. Healing Prayers: Prophetic Prayers that Brings Healing

6. Healing WORDS: Daily Confessions & Declarations to Activate Your Healing.

7. Prayers That Break Curses and Spells and Release Favors and Breakthroughs.

8. 120 Powerful Night Prayers That Will Change Your Life Forever.

9. How to Pray for Your Children Everyday

10. How to Pray for Your Family

11. Daily Prayer Guide

12. Make Him Respect You: 31 Very Important Relationship Advice for Women to Make their Men Respect them.

13. How to Cast Out Demons from Your Home, Office & Property

14. Praying Through the Book of Psalms

15. The Students' Prayer Book

16. How to Pray and Receive Financial Miracle

17. Powerful Prayers to Destroy Witchcraft Attacks.

18. Deliverance from Marine Spirits

19. Deliverance From Python Spirit

20. Anger Management God's Way

21. How God Speaks to You

22. Deliverance of the Mind

23. 20 Commonly Asked Questions About Demons

24. Praying the Promises of God

25. When God Is Silent! What to Do When Prayer Seems Unanswered or Delayed

26. I SHALL NOT DIE: Prayers to Overcome the Spirit and Fear of Death.

27. Praise Warfare

28. Prayers to Find a Godly Spouse

29. How to Exercise Authority Over Sickness

30. Under His Shadow: Praying the Promises of God for Protection (Book 2).

NOTES

About the Author

Daniel Chika Okpara is an influential voice in contemporary Christian ministry. His mandate is to make lives better through the teaching and preaching of God's Word with signs and wonders.

He is the presiding pastor of Shining Light Christian Centre, a fast-growing Church in the city of Lagos, and the president, Better Life World Outreach Center, a non-denominational ministry dedicated to global evangelism and prayer revival. He is also the founder of Breakthrough Prayers Foundation (www.breakthroughprayers.org), an online portal leading people all over the world to encounter God and change their lives through prayer. Every day, thousands of people use the Breakthrough Prayers Portal to pray, and hundreds of testimonies from all around the world are received through it.

He is a foremost Christian teacher and author whose books are in high demand in prayer groups, Bible studies, and for personal devotions. He has authored over 50 life-transforming books and manuals on business, prayer, relationship and victorious living, many of which have become international best-sellers.

He is a Computer Engineer by training and holds a Master's Degree in Christian Education from Cornerstone Christian University. He is married to Doris Okparam and they are blessed with lovely children.

Made in United States
North Haven, CT
03 May 2024